John Gaudioso's first venture into publishing has produced three children's stories. *Smoky, Smoky's Adventure,* and *Smoky to the Rescue*. Under current development is his latest in the *Smoky* series, titled, *Uptown – Not*.

Three Weeks, a Lie is his memoir; an autobiography. It provides detailed recollections, entombed for years, in deep recesses of John's mind. Myriad adjustments, memories, and recollections of his past often tormenting, distracting, and affecting family, friendships, and careers, amplifies remarkable courage and resilience experienced by a mother and her three children throughout their years of isolation, loneliness, and confusion.

Dedicated
to
mom,
Al, and Bob

John Gaudioso

THREE WEEKS, A LIE

MY MEMOIR

AUSTIN MACAULEY PUBLISHERS™

LONDON • CAMBRIDGE • NEW YORK • SHARJAH

Ordering Information:
Quantity sales: special discounts are available on quantity purchases by corporations, associations, and others. For details, contact the publisher at the address below.

Publisher's Cataloging-in-Publication data
Gaudioso, John
Three Weeks, a Lie

ISBN 9781645362869 (Paperback)
ISBN 9781645362876 (Hardback)
ISBN 9781645368748 (ePub e-book)

Library of Congress Control Number: 2020912799

www.austinmacauley.com/us

First Published (2020)
Austin Macauley Publishers LLC
40 Wall Street, 28th Floor
New York, NY 10005
USA

mail-usa@austinmacauley.com
+1 (646) 512 5767

Al and Bob
No doubt, wondering—John's writing a memoir!

My fear
Had I not written it
It would remain buried in a deep recess of my mind.

Their inputs, encouragements, and patience
made *My Memoir* a reality.

Nevertheless, I take full responsibility for the enclosed contents, recorded to
the best of my recollections.

Tables of Contents

MOM
Anna Rose Gaudioso

Prologue
Men in White

The year was 1947. Al was eight years old. I was seven years old. Bob was five and a half years old. Unfortunately, I'm the only one of us to clearly recall the intrusion by the Men in White.

They entered our apartment. They were in our hallway, heading toward our kitchen. Dad was expecting them. Mom didn't have a clue!

I heard Mom's voice. "Who are you?" "What's going on?" "Why are they here, Dominic?" None of it was making sense to me. Al, Bob, and I hugged close to each other, against our living room wall. Al has a vague memory of the intrusion. Bob has no recollection of it. *Unfortunately, I remember it all too well. After all, we had ringside seats.*

The Men in White reappeared. They were dragging Mom through our narrow hallway. Mom's cursing filled the air. "Dominic, stop them." She begged the Men in White to let her go. She called out for us. "Dominic, where are my babies?" Mom argued and yelled repeatedly, "Let me go. Where are you taking me? Who are you?" Her cries and yelling filled the apartment as she was dragged away by the Men in White. She cursed Dad.

Mom was angry and frightened. She was no match for the Men in White. Dad followed behind as Mom was dragged, half carried, out of our apartment, in full view of us. Dad didn't look in our direction. "What the hell."

Did anyone realize we were in the living room? Dad had to know. Of course, he had to know. Who else could have positioned us up against our living room wall? Were we part of this scenario? Was our presence supposed to make Mom cooperative?

Mom looked in our direction. We locked eyes. Tears flowed down her face. Her eyes were wide, filled with fear. It is a moment that remains etched into my mind to this day. The Men in White and Mom were out of our apartment. She was transferred to Brooklyn's Bellevue Hospital to a mental ward. I was confused.

It wasn't over. Within several weeks, Dad arranged for Al, Bob, and me to be transferred to an orphanage, under the guise of being transferred to a Special School. Mom and the three of us, Al, Bob, and me, were separated from each other. Mom was gone from us. We were gone from Mom.

What happened to our family?

Chapter One

Mom, Dad, John, Bob, and Al
Brooklyn, New York, 1946

Flatbush Avenue, Brooklyn, New York
1943–1947

A Few Good Years

Ah, we were a family then. Dad, Mom, Al, Bob, and me. We lived in an apartment at 1533 Flatbush Avenue, close to where Flatbush and Norstand avenues intersected each other.

Neighborhood

Our apartment was located on the second floor of a two-storied building. A hallway separated the entrance to our apartment and our playroom aka, our boy-cave. Our playroom was at the end of a hallway across from the main entrance to our apartment. Hours, surrounded with collections of toys, comic books, baseball cards, baseball gloves, bats, and balls; you name it, we had it all. Most times the doors to our playroom and apartment were left open. Dad whistled from within our apartment when we were called for supper, baths, bedtime, or in general.

A small bathroom was located on the left wall as you entered our apartment. Passing the bathroom, led to a small kitchen area. It was tight, housing a refrigerator, a washer with rubber rollers attached to the top where water from wet clothes were squeezed out.

A small gas stove, complete with an oven, was located against the wall near our kitchen window. A wash sink was located next to the oven. A small space under the sink held soaps, detergents, brushes, and washcloths.

Cabinetry along the floor were filled with pots, pans, and provided temporary housing for resident mice. A small Formica table surrounded with chairs completed our kitchen. Five of us crowded around that table for meals. It was tight.

The kitchen window opened to our rear fire escape offering a view from our fire escape facing rear fire escapes from buildings across from our apartment building. Clotheslines between our buildings stretched across backyards separating the rear of both buildings. Sometimes Mom stored milk bottles, eggs, cheeses, and butter on our windowsill, mostly in winter months.

A wall separated our kitchen from the living room. Our bedroom was separated from Dad and Mom's bedroom by a half wall, leaving an opening between the bedrooms. Their bedroom was large, with two large windows, overlooking Flatbush Avenue. On our side of the wall, Al and I shared a bed. Bob's crib was pushed up against the wall separating our bedrooms.

I remember watching Bob standing in his crib, holding on to a railing with one hand, while peeing through crib railings onto the wall. His pee dripped down the wall to an electrical outlet. Dad went a little nut. Funny!

Many an afternoon was spent peering out Dad and Mom's bedroom windows. I was transfixed for hours gazing down onto stores and pedestrian traffic on Flatbush Avenue. The A&P grocery store, a forerunner of one-stop super markets was a main attraction. Shoppers from nearby neighborhoods, arrived in trolley cars, buses, and subways.

In those early stages of one-stop shopping concepts, small businesses continued successfully for many years to come, selling fresh products from butcher, fish, and bakery shops throughout neighborhoods.

Not to be outdone, depending on the seasons, peddlers with horse-drawn carts jockeyed between trolley cars and buses, competing for customers from apartment buildings and pedestrians. They called out their specialties; blocks of ice, vegetables, fruit, blue coal chips, and knife sharpening to name a few.

Across from the A&P grocery store, almost directly below our apartment was an appliance store; featuring twelve-inch black and white television sets inserted into huge oversized consoles. It was a main attraction. Television was catching on big with the public. Broadcasts featuring news, westerns, and kid programs, all in black and white were initial first steps in television viewing.

The appliance store had huge windows which displayed television sets, with sound from T.V. programs hooked into speakers outside the store. A very good selling effort, attracting adults and children; causing crowds to gather on sidewalks opposite the windows to view and listen to T.V. programs.

Inside, standing next to the T.Vs, were grinning salesman. They smiled as they gestured to adults to come inside for a personal review. Children like Al and I were regular viewers alongside adults. Salesmen ignored us. We weren't waved in for a personal review.

It was there, I think; the idea of becoming a salesman began to interest me. I mean, we're outside, standing in the cold while salesmen inside dressed in suits and ties were smiling at us. In spite of the coldest winter days, we were bundled head to toe standing with older people, transfixed by what was being broadcast; News shows, cowboy movies and cartoons.

Backyard Activities

Fire escapes had many uses. Spring, summer, and fall months encouraged neighborhood apartment dwellers to take refuge on their fire escapes. Spring season was looked forward to, especially after a harsh winter.

Spring plantings of flowers and herbs, vegetables, cucumbers, tomatoes, lettuce, eggplant, and peppers followed. Seedlings planted in small pots, kept on fire escapes were transferred to backyard garden areas, located between rear facing buildings.

Fig trees were stripped of winter coverings, tar paper, burlap and a pail stacked on the top. Young fig trees bent into the soil and covered with inches of dirt were cleared, releasing branches to the open spring air. In late June ripened figs attracted birds to feast on them. Gardeners and birds picked ripened figs as fast as they could.

High above the gardens, spring weather reintroduced hanging wet clothes out to dry on clotheslines attached between fire escapes opposite rear building. A colorful mosaic of shirts, pants, underwear, and dresses danced in the wind throughout spring and fall seasons. The fresh smell of clothes removed from clotheslines was intoxicating.

Winter months invited freezing rains, creating eerie ice-coated clotheslines with icicles dripping from them. Occasionally, stiff shirts and pants hung could be seen.

Throughout spring, summer, and fall months, families sat on fire escapes and rooftops. Voices spoken in broken English and Italian echoed throughout backyards. Women exchanged gossip, new additions to families, shopping hints, updates on children, and who moved out and who moved into the neighborhood.

Summer months welcomed the familiar rings of Good Humor ice cream trucks and vendors, selling Italian Ices and multi-flavored sodas. Radios broadcasting baseball games, The Brooklyn Dodgers, New York Yankees, and The Giants, attracted men and kids rooting for their favorite teams. Programs featured 'The Green Hornet' and 'The Fat Man' to name a few.

Elderly Italian families listened to programs featuring Italian soap operas. Kids looked forward to summer camps, playgrounds, beaches, summer sport activities. 'Stickball,' 'Kick the Can,' 'Johnny on the Pony,' and 'Stoop Ball' were popular. Life was simple.

Fall season announced summer's end. It was time for kids to prepare for another year of schooling; Math, English, History, and tests were upon them. Being promoted to the next grade level was a priority for everyone, especially parents. Kids who got out of line in school, on the playground, or in a fight became victims to the clothesline connection. They never had a chance!

Family Activities
Telling Time

Dad gathered us around him. He produced a plastic clock. He rotated the long and short arms to numbered positions, beginning with hourly times, graduating to half hour and quarter hour times. Once we had it down, he moved arms straight up and down indicating hours and half hours. Each of us took turns repeating forward and backward times. By the time Mom returned to our apartment, we had learned to tell time. Dad bragged on us to Mom. It made me feel good.

Fighting the Japanese

Dad played a war game with us. We were fighting the Japanese. He knew a thing or two, since he was responsible for winning the Second World War, singlehanded, I might add. What's a war? We knew zip about wars. But we did know Dad beat the Japanese singlehandedly.

Later years, while researching Dad's military records, I came across documents, one indicating a Noncom rating, another with an officer's rank of Captain. I don't have a clue which one is true. But, I do know the closest Dad came to fighting the Japanese in World War II was from Mitchell Air Field, on Long Island, now home to Nassau University. Dad was assigned to inventory stores. He was responsible for maintaining various military inventory issued to airmen stationed at Mitchell Air Field.

Back to fighting the Japanese. "Boys, the Japs are coming." What were Japanese? We didn't care. We wanted to help Dad win the war – again! Dad arranged couches and chairs opposite each other. Dad directed us into positions facing each other in our living room aka, battlefield. He and Al were the GIs. Bob and I were the Japanese. We faced each other across 'no man's land.'

Dad made guns from pieces of wood removed from wooden crates. He attached thumbtacks at the front and rear barrel. A double-stretched rubber ban was fashioned between the tacks. Dad passed out ammo – small squares of cardboard. They were slipped between the rubber bands. Releasing the rubber band from the rear tack sent the ammo flying. Dad and Al were 'the good guys.' Bob and I were doomed.

Once settled in, a shout from Dad initiated a frenzy of cardboard 'ammo' flying across 'no man's land.' We ducked incoming cardboard as best we could. Bob and I received multiple hits. We were wounded. Our ammo ran out. Somehow, we hung in there.

Dad called a truce. He asked if we wanted to surrender. We were on the verge of surrendering when Dad shouted for us to retrieve spent ammo from no man's land as fast as we could. We bumped into each other, avoiding Dad, who had a jump on us.

Even though Bob and I were wounded, we kept at it. Dad was jumping, shooting, laughing, and shouting all sorts of military language. He shot cardboard ammo like it was going out of style. He may have been working off Al's pile. Bob and I continued being hit multiple times. I'm not sure we hit Dad or Al – well, maybe Al. Eye goggles! Don't be silly. Bob and I ran out of ammo. We surrendered. Dad and Al continued firing on us. We laid as low as we could until they ran out of ammo. Once again the GIs were victorious. America was safe. You can thank our dad.

Sundays with Dad and Mom

Sunday mornings following Mass, Dad collected a baseball, glove, and a bat from our playroom. Each of us carried a bat, ball, or glove. Dad smoked Camel cigarettes as we walked to the playground. On weekends, the playground gates were unlocked from eight in the morning through 12 noon. On the way, Dad gave us his usual pep talk. He was calm before the storm!

Dad preferred a regular baseball over a Spalding high-bounce ball, used by some of the boys. He pitched to Al. Bob was behind the plate, I was in the outfield. Al's occasional hits to the outfield were followed by encouraging shouts from Dad as I chased after the ball. "Throw it to me, Johnny." Needless to say, my throws were off the mark; making several bounces before reaching Dad.

While hitting the ball was fun for us. It wasn't for Dad. We'd swing at anything, over our heads, off a bounce, anywhere within a couple of feet of us. Often followed by "What are you swinging at?" When we did manage to hit the ball, it was destined to be hit away from whoever played in the outfield. "Geez, Louise," shouted Dad!

Many missed hits to all parts of the outfield including foul balls hit over a webbed barb wired fence. The balls bounced toward curbsides, occasionally hitting a car. Dad asked strangers, even owners of cars hit by a bouncing baseball, to toss it back to him, as he apologized.

At some point, Dad called it a day. Dad muttered to no one in particular as we collected our one glove, baseball, and bat. We tried our best not to upset Dad. Sometimes we were on – most times – not! We were seven, six, and five years old respectively. When we did make contact with the bat, catch a hit ball, or hustle after a ball, Dad was encouraging. "That's the ticket. Now we're getting somewhere."

Garden Discovery

While wandering through the playground, I spotted boys and girls planting in a garden area enclosed with fencing. I approached an open gate to the garden. The garden had long rows with vegetables, flowers, and herbs growing. Kids were kneeling, planting, and weeding along the rows. A lady walked between the rows, stopping once in a while to speak with them. I remained by the opened gate. The lady noticed me standing, staring at them.

She smiled and motioned me to her. She took my hand into hers. We continued walking through the rows of growing flowers, vegetables, and herbs. She encouraged the kids as we walked past them.

She led me to a row of string beans. It wasn't long before I was picking string beans alongside her, placing them in a basket as we moved along the row. Once in a while she smiled at me as we picked along the rows of string beans. I was having fun. The smell of growing vegetables overwhelmed me. I wanted to grow vegetables.

The lady supervised the garden area. I've long lost her name. Besides, it was unpronounceable for me. The garden belonged to the neighborhood kids. They were responsible for tending whatever they grew. Whatever they grew was theirs to take home.

Dad was calling for me. We had to go home. She asked if I would like to grow vegetables. Was she kidding? I was hooked. I jumped at the opportunity. She led me to an area where a row of string beans were recently planted. Some were beginning to spout. She said they needed someone to care for them. "Would you like to care for them?"
"You bet." They became my string beans.

Throughout the remaining summer months I harvested 'lots' of string beans. I managed to visit my garden as often as I could throughout the week. On Sundays, after practicing baseball with Dad and my brothers, Dad let me visit my garden. I watered them and picked ripen string beans to take home for Mom.

When I showed up with fresh picked string beans, Mom smiled 'that special smile.' She'd prepare them in a tomato sauce, mixed with garlic, oil, and salt and pepper. Sometimes, she prepared a cold salad with the string beans topped off with wine vinegar, salt, and pepper. Yummy! I'm forever grateful to have met the lady in that garden. Today gardening remains a priority, providing me hours of silence, solitude, and calmness.

Locked 'In'!

One Sunday, as we were leaving the playground, we found the gates locked. The security guard was nowhere to be found. We were stuck inside the playground. Dads were upset. The men mumbled, smoked cigarettes, and attempted to calm the kids down. The only option was to climb over the gate's iron railings. The iron railings ended with pointed tops. Hello!

Men climbed over iron railings. A sickening feeling developed in the pit of my stomach. The pointed, iron railings were almost as tall as the men. As far as I was concerned it could have been twenty feet high. I didn't want to climb over them.

With men safely over the iron railings; boys lined up waiting for their turn to climb over the iron railings. One by one, kids were assisted by men reaching through the railings. One by one, kids were lifted up and over the iron railings.

I kept positioning behind boys lined up for their climb over the pointed iron railings. Each time I heard Dad call out for me, I backed up to the end of the line. Eventually, I was the last boy standing. Al, Bob, and Dad were calling to me from the other side of the iron railings.

I stared at the pointed iron railings for a long time. My stomach was in an uproar. Dad was encouraging. "Come on, Johnny. It's OK. I'll help you across." Was this Dad? Not yelling! 'Did he take nice pills?' Then again, he had an audience. A few adults and some kids on the other side of the railing called out. "Come on, kid. Climb over the fence." Fence! Did they see what I was staring at? There wasn't a fence. There was an iron railing with pointed tips.

I approached the railing for my climb. Encouraging voices surrounded from the 'other side' calling for me to climb the 'fence,' really? Hands reached through railings, grabbing me, thrusting me magically up and over the pointed iron railings. "Atta boy, Johnny" Dad called out. I was safely deposited at his feet. I may have peed my pants!

Ah, the walk home! That was the best. Walking home with Dad through the neighborhood was relaxing. Dad was calm. He'd throw a baseball a few feet in front of us. We chased after it. We tossed it back to him. Dad, a cigarette hanging from his lips, offered advice on how to field and hit baseballs.

Dad was all of five feet and a few inches tall. He sported a trimmed moustache, matching straight jet-black hair. His swagger set him apart from others. He was raised by immigrant parents in the streets of Brooklyn's Italian neighborhoods.

He was a young man, the father of three boys, married to Mom, a beautiful woman several years his junior. In our eyes, he was 'this magical dad.' He could do anything.

Mom's Italian Gravy

Mom prepared a traditional Italian meal. Meatballs, hot and sweet sausages, and a piece of pork, when she could get it! Everything was browned in oil and fresh garlic. They were added to herbs and homegrown tomatoes to simmer over a low heat into a rich red tomato gravy. The smell Mom's gravy joined with neighboring Italian families preparing their Sunday meals was intoxicating. "OMG!"

Mom's cooking skills matched our grandmothers and aunts from both sides of our families. The absolute best home-prepared traditional Italian meals were prepared in their kitchens. To this day, those Italian prepared meals remain the best I've ever enjoyed.

Our pace quickened as we neared Flatbush Avenue. Once across, we raced to our apartment. Al usually won. I was always right behind him. Bob walked with Dad. Entering our apartment, we were overwhelmed by the smell of Mom's gravy, simmering in a large pot, on the stove. We made beeline to the kitchen where Mom was preparing supper.

She greeted us as we rushed in with "Boys, wash your hands. We'll be eating soon." Dad followed, heading straight for the kitchen. Mom greeted him with a kiss and, usually, a corner piece of Italian bread, dipping with gravy. Their laughs were reassuring. Most likely, Dad related a story about us, causing Mom to laugh. I wonder if he shared our climbs over pointed iron railing? Probably. This was a happy memory.

Sunday Meals with Family Relatives

Aside from Sunday dinners at home, dinners with family relatives was special. Aunts, uncles, and cousins gathered together. Traditional Italian pasta meals and salads were served. Salad was served first, followed by penne pasta. Meatballs, hot and sweet sausage, and pork completed the first part of our meals.

Cousins were seated at a small table off to the side. Adults made themselves comfortable around the big table. Mom made sure our plates were filled with pasta and meats. She returned to our uncles and aunts, singing out to us, "Let me know if you need more."

Uncles and aunts helped themselves to plates, some with a bit more of their favorite meats added to their plates. Laughter, low voices, in Italian or English were exchanged, with glances in our direction, assuring, we didn't overhear what they were discussing. We were only interested in eating.

Following our meal, men eased back into chairs and couches, resting, drinking wine, smoking, and napping. They unhooked their belts and the first button on their pants, in order to better digest their food; making room for Italian pastries.

Aunts cleared the table of plates, utensils, glasses, and leftovers. Everything was carried to the kitchen sink. Aunts washed, dried, and put plates and glasses into cabinets. They reset tables. Coffee espresso, Anisette, B&B, and brandy were served with Italian pastries and assorted home-baked Italian cookies.

Us kids? We played in any cleared area, usually in the living room where the men were resting. Occasionally, someone would request one of us to empty an ashtray, refresh a glass of wine. Whatever it was, we were glad to be included. Everyone feasted on Italian treats and cookies, that is, after uncles and aunts removed their favorites from the trays. Our favorites were anything left in the trays.

Sunday Walks Along Flatbush Avenue

Following a traditional Sunday Italian meal, and depending on the weather, we'd stroll along Flatbush Avenue. Al took off walking ahead us. He was a fast walker, leading the way. Reaching a corner, he'd peek back for Dad to motion him when it was safe to cross the street. Bob and I walked alongside of Dad and Mom.

Dad and Mom walked arm in arm talking, laughing, and occasionally speaking to us as we enjoyed a Sunday afternoon walk along Flatbush Avenue. Dad and Mom made sure to stop at a candy store along the way. We'd be treated to an egg cream soda to share. Mom made sure we saved some of the egg cream soda for Al.

Returning from our Sunday walk, to our apartment, we settled in our living around Dad. We listened to the radio, mostly, to a baseball game or to music. When listening to a baseball game, Dad explained plays, named batters, and applauded good plays or a hit. Dad played an important role in our understanding the game of baseball. His favorite team was the Brooklyn Dodgers. If they weren't playing, he switched to the Giants or the New York Yankees. Al rooted for the Yankees. Go figure! Dad, Bob, and I were Dodger fans.

Leftovers

Mom prepared leftovers, meatballs, sausages, and pasta for our Sunday night supper. All the leftovers filled a large frying pan. Everything was fried in oil, salt, and pepper. It was the best tasting leftover meal you can imagine.

Ice Cream My Treat!
Playground

I was playing stickball with friends. I heard the familiar ringing bells of the Good Humor ice cream truck. I led everyone to the arriving ice cream truck. Boys circled around the ice cream man, ordering their favorite ice cream. I didn't realize what was happening. They thought I was treating them to ice cream. Really! The ice cream man smiled at me as I ordered my ice cream. He handed it to me, saying. It was free. Free! A funny feeling was growing in my stomach as I reached for my money to pay for my ice cream treat. The smile on the ice cream man's face disappeared.

With melting ice cream dripping onto my hands, I paid for my ice cream. The ice cream man stared at me, saying, "Somebody has to pay for the ice creams." Oops! A few boys paid up. Others didn't have money or wouldn't pay. Regardless, everyone continued enjoying their ice creams. Little by little, boys began inching away from me and the ice cream man.

The ice cream man called over a playground counselor. They huddled together, occasionally looking in my direction. I managed to continue eating my ice cream. Hey, it was melting.

The counselor asked why I told the boys to order ice cream. I responded. "I didn't tell them to do that." He seemed confused. The counselor asked if my parents were at the playground. I answered, "No." He took down my name and address. I was doomed. The ice cream man wanted to be paid for the ice cream. The counselor ended up paying for the ice creams.

Dad and Mom never mentioned the incident. My punishment came in another way. For several days, I avoided the playground. I couldn't visit my garden plot.

Ice Cream Snack
with Dad and Mom

We were tucked in for the night. I got up to pee. On my way to the bathroom I saw Dad and Mom sitting together on the couch in our living room, eating ice cream. Where did they get ice cream? I finished peeing. I headed back to bed. Dad motioned me to them. Mom handed me a spoon filled with ice cream. It was delicious vanilla ice cream. One spoon full and I was off to bed. It was a special moment for me.

Al's Nailed Down

We had a wooden toy chest. It held our toys and, on occasion, Al removed the toys and climbed into the toy chest. He wanted to tell us a story. He'd close the lid and...slowly emerging with a spooky story which scared the be-gees out of Bob and me.

Once when Al was inside the toy chest, preparing to scare the crap out of us, I took a few nails and a hammer from Dad's toolbox. I sat on the toy chest and hammered a few nails into the toy chest. Bob watched, not saying a word. Al was pushing up on the lid and yelling..."Open the lid!" I got off the toy chest. I sat in front of it laughing. It was funny. I nailed Al into the toy chest.

Dad's whistle from the kitchen interrupted us. He was signaling supper was ready. Bob streaked for the kitchen. I followed him. We stopped to wash our hands in the bathroom before sitting at the table for supper. Dad asked. "Where's Al?"
Bob volunteered, "He's in the toy chest."
I was dead meat. Thanks, Bob.

"What do you mean?" bellowed Dad as he got up from the table. "What is he doing in the toy chest?" Dad called on his way to our playroom.

"John nailed him in the toy chest." Geez Bob, can ya give me break. My attention shifted from supper to finding a hiding place. I got up from the table. Mom began peppering me with questions. I took off, heading for 'the springs.'

Dad's voice was loud, clear, and scary. "He nailed Al in the toy chest?" His voice reached my inner soul. Dad removed the nails from the lid. There weren't that many. Al made his way to the table. Mom provided a few words of encouragement to him.

Bed Springs

Al was safe, back in the world of the living. By this time, I settled into hiding under their bed, searching for a good position. I laid on my back, grabbing onto bedsprings tightly. I waited for Dad. I knew the drill. So did he. He arrived with Mom's broom stick. He called out. "You better come out now, while you can." I took that to mean 'I need to tighten my grip to the bed springs.'

Dad searched for my body with the stick end of the broom. He was on his knees, shoving the broomstick in all directions. Sort of like American ships in WWII discharging depth bombs into the water searching for German Submarines. Eventually, he worked the stick close to me. I held on to the springs, moving in all directions, doing my best not to get hit.

Hiding under the bed wasn't really hiding. Aside from leaving the apartment, it was the only place I could hide. Dad knew this. Sometimes, knowing I couldn't move from where I was hiding, he'd take his time before coming after me. In time, I'd learned to contort my body, avoiding his probing. Sometimes it took Dad a while to locate me. Not this time! He was pissed, really pissed. He made contact. I wailed out loud.

This was Mom's clue. Once she heard my wailing, she did what she always did, yelling for Dad to stop. "Dominic, stop before you kill him." Dad, uttering a string of threats, in Italian, withdrew the broomstick, saying for the hundredth time. "One of these days, I'll knock you from here to Carnarsie. You better straighten up." Eventually, I learned Carnarsie wasn't too far from where we lived on Flatbush Avenue.

With a final shove with a probing broomstick, Dad returned to the kitchen for his supper. I remained under the bed. This was normal. It gave Dad time to settle down. I waited until I heard the radio playing music, a baseball game or a favorite radio program. Once Dad was comfortable, smoking a Camel cigarette with Al and Bob playing nearby, I knew Mom would be calling to me to come out from under the bed.

Dad generally got over his anger in a short amount of time. This time, he took a little longer. Mom fetched me from under the bed. I clung to her as we headed to the kitchen. As we passed through the living room, I hugged to the side not facing Dad.

I wouldn't look in his direction. Dad had a stare like a laser beam. It could freeze me in my tracks. He offered a few words of advice to me as we passed him. Mom settled me down. I ate my supper. I was bruised, I was fed. I was alive. Al wasn't hurt. I hated Bob.

Al's Nose Job

Once again playing in our playroom, I managed to hold Al down while shoving chucks of soft wonder bread into his nose. Al broke loose. He ratted me out to Mom, Mom hollered for me come to the kitchen. Al was sitting in a chair while she removed wonder bread from his nose. "You wait until your father gets home." Mom was upset. Once Al's nose was cleared of bread stuffing, he was up and out. Mom let me know in so many words 'not to ever do that again.' The matter was closed.

Crayon Incident

Mom punished me by having me sit in the kitchen at our small table reading from one of the schoolbooks I was permitted to take home for reading lessons. The books were the property of the Catholic school. We checked them out. When we checked them back in, Sisters inspected them for drawings or any other marks which shouldn't be there.

This particular book had pictures throughout it. The pictures were outlined in black lines. They were more attractive than reading the words. I had a crayon. I began coloring in the drawings on each page. We weren't permitted to write and draw on the pages much less color crayons to the drawings. I turned a page and colored it. I was deep into coloring when Mom interrupted me. "John, are you coloring with those crayons?" She lost it. She forgot about 'soft bread stuffed up Al's nose.'

Mom ripped the book away from me. She turned page after page, exposing colored drawings. Mom was upset. She was shaking the book at me. Colored drawings flashed before my eyes. I knew I was in doo-doo, really deep doo-doo. Dad and Mom would be expected to pay for the book. They didn't have a penny to spare. Mom came up with a solution. "You take that book back to school. You get rid of it. Do you hear me! Get rid of it." she screamed.

I asked her. "What do I do?"

Mom went ballistic. "If you bring that marked up book back home, you'll deal with Dad. Do you hear me?" I heard Mom, real good. Loud and clear. There was no way I was going to bring that book back home. That much I was sure of. I understood completely.

Once in class, my eyes went to bookshelves, where class books are stored. Copies of my book was there. It called out to me. When Sister was otherwise occupied, I exchanged my marked-up book for an unmarked copy.

I gave the unmarked book to Mom. She opened it, turning the pages, searching for 'my art work.' She handed the book back to me, smiling! Mom didn't ask me how I was able to get an unmarked book. Mom didn't mention it or Al's stuffed nose to Dad. I escaped punishment on both counts.

On the Steps with Dad

Dad didn't smoke cigars in our apartment. He'd sit on the top step of the stairs, just outside the door to our apartment. Sometimes I'd sit with him. He was easy to be with when enjoying a cigarette or a cigar.

Once Dad showed me how to suck a raw egg. He pecked small holes in the top and bottom of the eggshell. Then he sucked the raw egg completely out of its shell. OK, my turn. Dad got another egg. He made the openings and passed the egg to me. I sucked the raw egg out from the shell. I liked the taste of the yoke. Another time, Dad was eating pickled pigs bones from a jar. I watched him gnawing the meat from the bones. He let me have some. I liked the taste of the pickled pig bones. I still do.

Sledding with Dad

We had a big sled. It supported the three of us. Dad lugged it from our playroom to the street. He pulled us through snow-covered streets throughout our neighborhood. Kids welcomed us by throwing snowballs at us. Dad could have pulled us past them. Not Dad. That would have been easy! He pulled the sled to the side, unloaded us and yelled, "Get behind the sled, boys. Start making snowballs for me." We huddled down and made snowballs as fast as we could. Dad exchanged snowballs with the kids.

Snowballs were flying in both directions. Dad was laughing, having fun, throwing snowballs as fast as we could make them. A few kids joined us. They made snowballs, passing them to Dad. Now, we threw snowballs back at kids. Everyone was throwing, laughing, ducking, and yelling for more snowballs to toss. Dad saw an opening. "OK, men, get on the sled."

Dad got us out of Dodge. Nice memory!

Prospect Park Lake Swimming Lessons

Dad rented a rowboat. We sat on slats, as close together as possible. He rowed out to the middle of the lake. "OK, Johnny, get in the water. Hang on to the back of the boat."

"What?"

"Johnny, you're going learn to swim; it's easy. Kick your feet."

I jumped into the water and worked my way along the side of it to the back the rowboat. I held on to the rowboat. Dad told me to kick legs. I did. "Take your hands off the boat, Johnny."

That wasn't gonna happen, no way. I wasn't letting go of the boat. "Okay, let go of one hand, Johnny." I did. I was OK so long as I had one hand on the rear of the rowboat. "Take both of your hands off the boat, Johnny." I didn't. After several attempts, Dad gave up. I climbed back into the boat, wet and avoiding Dad. Al and Bob weren't required to learn how to swim? Geez!

Al's 'Almost' Baseball Glove Purchase

The baseball-glove request is a classic. Al asked Dad if he could buy one. I don't know what he was thinking. After all our baseball 'try outs' with Dad, batting and chasing after baseballs in the park on Sunday mornings, did Al think Dad would spring for a new glove?

Dad gave in. He didn't realize the baseball glove Al was interested in cost almost five dollars. Al didn't tell the cost to Dad. Five dollars in 1947 was a lot of money. Dad give Al a five-dollar bill with strict instructions to bring him the change. Al was off to buy a brand-new baseball glove.

Al returned with a brand-new baseball glove. He fished out change from his pocket to give to Dad. Dad went berserk. Paying five dollars for a baseball glove wasn't gonna happen.

Al was sent back to the store. He would return the glove and bring Dad his five dollars. Somehow, Al managed to make the exchange. He returned the five dollars to Dad. He was disappointed. Dad was relieved. Eventually, Dad came up with an old beat-up baseball glove for us to share on Sunday mornings.

Submarine

A Movie Tone News reel clip played at intermission at a Saturday matinee featuring a Navy submarine diving through waves, disappearing, and resurfacing. I was hooked. I asked Dad for a toy submarine. OK, OK, I 'begged' Dad for a toy submarine. Dad and Mom surprised me, buying it for my birthday.

Dad and I were on a mission. Dad was taking me to a store where all kinds of toys were sold. They sold toy submarines, army tanks, airplanes, you name it – they had it. It was a cold day in January. Dad was in a good mood. I'd raced ahead every few feet. He'd run up catching me by my collar. When he released me, I ran again. Dad in a heavy overcoat, scarf, and hat, racing after me. It would remain a special moment for me.

The man showed us the submarine. I was beside myself. I kept asking, "Is it like the real ones?" The man assured Dad, it dove and resurfaced just like a real submarine. I really wanted that submarine. Dad bought for me. I held it all the way home. The only other time I begged for a toy was from Mom. It was a six-shooter 'cap gun.' Mom nixed it. "Too dangerous, Johnny."

"Mom, it's a cap gun!" Geez!

The submarine was gray throughout the hull. Painted wood panels and hatches outlined the deck. A single gun was mounted in the rear of the submarine's conning tower. An American flag was painted on both sides of the submarine. Another American flag attached to a pole was inserted in the rear of the submarine. It was a special toy.

A cool thing about the submarine was that it was self-propelled. A wound up handle protruded from the deck. The propellers spun, sending the submarine in a dive, 'hunting for enemy ships.'

Throughout winter months, I'd float my submarine in our bathtub, mostly after we bathed, and depending on how dirty the water was. Sometimes, Mom let me float it in the kitchen sink. My submarine came with a long string to be attached to a small loop on the back of it. If for some reason, it didn't resurface on its own, it could be rescued by pulling on the string. When my submarine was on trial runs in our bathtub or kitchen sink, it didn't need to have the string attached to it.

Spring arrived. The weather was warm enough for Dad to take me to Prospect Park; to the same lake where he rented a rowboat and attempted to teach me how to swim! That was fun. The lake area was crowded with families. I may have been the only boy in Brooklyn with a toy submarine. Adults, boys, and girls were attracted to us. Dad smoked a camel cigarette while talking with adults.

After many test dives in our bathtub and kitchen sink, I was ready to launch my submarine on its first voyage in a real lake. Dad wound the handle tight. He held the submarine propeller with his fingers so they wouldn't spin until the submarine was in the water.

I was nervous and excited. Dad passed the submarine to me. "Go ahead, Johnny, put it in the water." I held on to my submarine with one hand and the propeller with my fingers just like Dad did. I had everyone's attention. It was show time. I dipped my submarine under the water. I knew from experience what to expect when I released my grip. My submarine soared off into the depths of the lake. Boys and girls, even adults, cheered. My submarine was patrolling the depths of a lake in Prospect Park, Brooklyn, New York.

I waited. We all waited. Men were smoking, looking out at where they thought the submarine would rise to the surface. I knew that it would. And, it did, to the roar of shouts of "Look, look, there it is." I was happy. Dad was happy. Everybody pointing to where my submarine surfaced.

Just as I knew it would, it dove back under the water, followed by more shouts of encouragements and laughter. Once again, fingers pointed to where my submarine would break the surface. After minutes of expectations, and my submarine not surfacing, I realized what was wrong.

"Dad, you forgot to tie the string to the loop hole." Dad looked down at me. He turned to the lake, staring out at the water, a cigarette hanging from his lips, seemly frozen in place. He realized what happened to my submarine. It was lost in a lake in Prospect Park.

Dad was cursing, before realizing he had an audience. Adults, mostly men, joined Dad with a few choice words of their own.

My submarine was lying at the bottom of the lake. I was a mess. Dad tried consoling me. "That's a first." Adults and kids extended tree branches into the water, trying to locate my submarine. Their search was in vain. Kids asked, "What happened to the submarine?" "Did it sink?" Dad was beside himself.

"It will come up." I knew different. It was over. I began to cry. A few men tried to console me. The crowd was retreating from the lake. Others hung around, hoping the submarine would float to the top. Kid's wondering out loud "Is it really a submarine?" "It's doing nothing!" "I don't want one."

I said to Dad, again, "You forgot to tie the string to the loop hole." Dad had this look when he was angry. He was really angry. His eyes became small. One smaller than the other. Weird. I was doomed. My crying continued. Dad fought with all his might to control himself. Thankfully, a few adults were still in the area. We left the lake. As we headed home on the Trolley Car, I went into sniff mode. "Don't worry, Johnny, I'll get another one for you." Yeah, sure, Dad!

If Dad attached the string to my submarine, I might have been able to pull it back to the shore. Dad forgot the string. I was guilty too. But, not as much as Dad. As soon as we entered our apartment, I raced up the stairs, through the door, shouting, and crying, "Mom, my submarine sank in the water. Dad forgot to bring the string. My submarine sank."

Dad voiced, "It wasn't my fault. He forgot to bring the string."

OK! "Who's the adult here?" Mom calmed us down. I pouted throughout the day

I'd mentioned the submarine incident to Jo Anne a number of times. She was on the lookout for an identical toy submarine. She found one in an antique store. Today it occupies a special space in my study.

Scrap Man

Scrap men were familiar sights in our neighborhood. Kids working for them searched alleyways for newspapers, wire hangers, toys, you name it, the scrap men wanted it. They paid kids based on what they found, mostly in nickels and dimes. Scrap men established routes in and around neighborhood apartments' buildings with alleyways.

I wanted to be a part of the scrap man who had a route in our neighborhood. I picked out a spot on his route where kids waited for him. I stood with them. He showed up. He selected two kids to run alongside his truck as he made his rounds, slowly passing apartment buildings. Kids ran into alleyways searching for newspapers, hangers, iron, whatever scraps they found, carrying it back to the scrap man.

To my surprise, he selected me. I didn't run ahead with the others. He told me to sit on the back of his truck. When he selected a spot to wait on whatever was found by runners, I was told to jump off to run in and out of alleyways.

Since I was alone, I didn't need to share collected scraps with anyone. I had good luck. I was fast. I didn't waste time. After a few times, hauling scrap from alleyways, he always selected me as an advance runner. He drove slowly with an eye out for me coming from an alleyway. I'd carry out whatever I could manage. I let him know when I left scraps behind before running ahead in search of scraps. Kids retrieved the scraps. I received credit for the find.

Scooter

I came across a scooter. I inspected it. It was beat up. The frame was rusted throughout. The rubber on the wheels were in good shape. I stood on the scooter. The wheels wobbled as I rolled it. But, it rolled. I wanted it. I thought of hiding it, coming back for it later.

I took a chance. I took it back to the truck. The scrap man could keep it. I couldn't stop him. I placed it carefully in the truck bed as far away from collected scraps. The scrap man turned, wanting to see what I had. He noticed the scooter. He never said a word. We finished the route. I slowly exited the rear of the truck, waiting for the usual payoff in dimes or nickels.

"You want that scooter, kid?"
"I sure do."
"You can take it. But, I won't pay you, OK?" I didn't care. I wanted that scooter. I pulled it off the back end of his truck. He smiled. I headed home with my broken down scooter.

I babied the scooter all the way home, afraid of something coming loose and falling off. The wheels rolled uneasily. But, they rolled. Once in a while I'd ride it for just a few feet before stepping off it. I was so excited. It was rusty and dirty. The rubber on the handlebars were missing exposing rusted iron handles. I wondered, did the scrap man notice the iron handles and frame? I'm sure he knew the value. He knew the scooter caught my attention. I was thankful for his decision.

I parked the scooter in our playroom. I didn't tell Mom. I waited for Dad to come home from work. I spent the entire time home in our playroom or sitting on the top of the steps waiting for Dad. The door to our apartment building opened. Dad was home.

He saw me and smiled as he climbed the stairs to our apartment. That was all I needed. I followed him into the kitchen where Mom was. He always went straight to Mom. He looked down at me standing near them. He wondered what was up!

I had to own up to how I came to find the scooter. I told Dad and Mom I sometimes gathered scraps for a scrap man. I took the scraps to his dilapidated old truck. "Everybody did it. He paid us." "No, I didn't know his name." It never occurred to me to ask him his name. In fact, I don't recall if he knew any of our names. He referred to us as "Hey, kid."

Mom wanted me to stop riding with him. It wasn't safe. I was on the verge of agreeing to stop riding with the scrap man, when Dad asked the ultimate question. How much was he paying me? I told them, it was loose change, nickels, dimes, sometimes pennies.

"What did I do with the money?" That was easy. I traded for baseball cards and comic books, which they knew were in our playroom. Dad was fine. "OK, be careful." Mom wasn't on board, but didn't press it. I continued working with the scrap man whenever I could, earning loose change.

The scooter received Dad's interest. He looked it over. He pointed out the rust, the wobbly wheels, and missing rubber from the handles. Dad was quiet for a bit before offering, "Johnny, are you sure you want to keep it? The scooter is rusted, hardly worth anything. What do you want to do with it?"

I replied, "I wanna fix it."

Dad came through, big time. Some nights, after supper, I watched as he worked on my scooter. He removed rust from the metal parts with sandpaper. He adjusted the wheels, applying oil to them until they were spinning without any effort at all. He re-secured the rear kickstand enabling the scooter to stand on its own.

I was beside myself. My feelings for Dad were at an all-time high. It was me and Dad, fixing my scooter. Well, mostly Dad, with me watching. The scooter was ready for finishing touches. Dad appeared with a small can of green paint. He had me wipe the entire scooter clean with towels. We were ready to paint my scooter. We were partners.

Dad laid out newspaper on the playroom floor. With a camel cigarette dangling from his lips, he painted the scooter with deep green paint. It looked brand new. My green scooter. My submarine was replaced.

I was so proud of having that scooter. I found it in a junk pile, in the rear of an alleyway, tossed away. A scrap man made it mine. Dad agreed to repair it. We worked together. I think in retrospect, Dad enjoyed working on the scooter, repairing it to an almost new.

I was restricted to riding on our block which was shaped like a triangle separated by three streets. It was an island. I must have ridden my green scooter around the block hundreds of times. I passed small businesses, storefronts, scooting in and around people as they went about their business. They smiled or waved as I'd scooter past them. "The wheels on the bus go round and round." I enjoyed riding that green scooter.

The Girl

Dad walked through the apartment door. 'What was he doing home in the afternoon?' I was with a girl, from the neighborhood. She was leaning against the wall next to the small radiator in the entrance hallway to our apartment. She was holding her dress up around her waist. Her panties were still on. We were staring at each other. We were curious!

Dad was standing there, with a puzzled look. He looked at the girl, then at me. He went into over drive mode. "What the hell?" The girl began crying while pulling her panties up. Dad yelled. "Stay right where you are" to her. I was already flying up the stairs. Good thing, my pants weren't down.

Dad flew up the stairs after me. He almost caught me. I flew into our apartment, passing Mom's bewildered look as I headed for the springs. I slid under the bed, turning my body, and grabbing onto bedsprings. I held on for dear life.
"What's going on, Dominic?" Mom shouted at Dad, as I imagined him grabbing a broomstick and heading to their bedroom. "That son of a bitch kid of yours." They began yelling at each other. Mom wanted to know what was going on. I hung on, knowing I was doomed. I heard Mom's voice, following Dad into their bedroom asking, "What's going on?"

Dad shouted, "I come home. Guess what? I see a girl holding her dress up with 'him' staring at her underwear."
"She was undressed?" Mom asked. "And John was with her?"
Dad responded, "They were both undressed in the entrance way." That wasn't true. My fly was open; but my pants were still up!

"Oh my God, Oh my God," Mom called out to no one in particular. Then to me. "Come out from there, do you hear me, Johnny? Come out this minute." I wasn't moving. "Where's the girl?" Mom yelled.

Dad yelled back "She's downstairs. I told her to stay there," which prompted a few more 'Oh my God's' from Mom. Mom left for the girl. Dad resumed searching for my gonads with the end of the broom. Mom returned yelling "Dominic, the girl's gone!" I was relieved, temporally at least. I positioned and struggled for better positions, preparing for the probing boom stick.

I had company. Staring at me through her yellow eyes was Penny, our cat. I couldn't tell if she was feeling sorry for me or was annoyed for the interruption. At any rate, she figured out the situation. She waited; one last look at me and she flew out from under the bed, passing Dad and Mom as they blessed Penny with a verbal assault. Penny made her escape.

Dad and Mom didn't get anywhere by questioning me while I hung on to bedsprings. They left me, knowing I wouldn't come out until some sort of truce was arranged. After they fed Al and Bob, Mom coaxed me out from under their bed. They hovered over me throughout supper. They peppered me with questions. Mom was crying. I said I was sorry at least a hundred times.

Dad went into detective mode, playing both roles – the good cop and the bad cop. "Johnny, what is the girl's name?" I didn't know. I guess I should have asked her before she pulled up her dress. Dad continued "Did she go to your school?" I didn't know. "How did you know her?"

"Is she from the neighborhood?" I didn't know. Dad went into bad cop mode. "How the hell can you be with a girl and not know her name?" Mom continued crying.

They finally tired of my answers. I was restricted from playing outside after school. I had to come directly home. I couldn't play in our playroom. Mom needed to keep an eye on me. As to the girl, I don't know how we ended up in the entrance hallway. It could have been her idea. Just saying.

Visiting Santa

Christmas was interesting. Mom took us to Macy's department store. We were gonna see Santa Claus. We arrived along with a zillion other boys and girls. Long lines greeted us, all waiting to see Santa Claus. Santa's helpers did the best they could, keeping excited boys and girls from peaking and moving in and out of lines to catch a glimpse of Santa Claus. He was perched on the top of a make-believe mountain with fake snow and Christmas trees.

Mothers were patiently keeping us in line as they spoke among themselves while keeping their eyes on us. Holiday music flowed throughout the store. Santa's helpers, dressed in red outfits and funny pointed hats assisted mothers and kids through the winding path to Santa. He promised toys for every good little boy and girl. He didn't really know me, did he?

We were in line with Mom who monitored us as best she could, telling us to behave or else! Finally, Mom had had it. She shooed us out of the line. I realized what she did. I became upset. "Aren't we going to see Santa Claus? I want to see Santa Claus." I became a pain in the royal butt. I'm sure Al and Bob were upset too.

Mom spoke with one of Santa's helpers. We were steered to another area where a 'second Santa' was seated in a large chair at the top of a fake mountain with fake Christmas trees and fake snow just like the first Santa Claus. A line of kids waiting to see Santa Claus formed at the bottom of the mountain. This Santa was different. He looked down to us, waived from his chair, shouting "HO-HO-HO! Merry Christmas." No kids were on his lap, or even close to him.

Santa's helpers waved presents at us from the top of the mountain. Mom said, we were going to receive a Christmas gift from Santa. First Mom needed to insert a coin into a red Christmas wrapped mailbox. After a few HO, HO, HOs from Santa, Our gift was sailing down a long slide. Santa gave us a coloring book.

Mom handed me the coloring book, pointing out, it was a magic coloring book. It came with a small paintbrush. I wasn't impressed. I handed it to Al. "I'll wait on the next Christmas gift."

Mom said, "The coloring book is for all of you."

Mom steered us to a water fountain. She opened the coloring book to a blank page. She wet the brush. She applied the wet brush to the blank page. Almost immediately, colors appeared, filling the blank page with pictures. It was magic! Colorful figures of Santa, Mrs. Claus, and Santa's helpers appeared. It was cool watching the different colors appearing on each page. Truth be said, we took turns and were through the entire coloring book in no time at all. Mom made us wave at Santa Claus as we left. I don't think he saw us.

Christmas Tree Shopping with Dad

Shopping for our Christmas tree with Dad was fun. He walked us to the florist shop, just up the corner at Flatbush and Norstand avenues about three storefronts down from our apartment. Christmas trees and wreaths were displayed along outside a floral shop. It was cold. Wind blew snowflakes in all directions.

Dad walked us, occasionally taking a drag from his camel cigarette, through tiny aisles lined with Christmas trees and wreaths. He was dressed in his overcoat and hat. "Stay close, boys" as we entered the area of Christmas trees. Dad was on a mission! From time to time he'd select a tree, pick it up, and shake it, giving it a good once over. After careful inspections made on several Christmas Trees, he whistled after us. Dad was standing, smiling next to the Christmas tree. "OK, boys, let's get around this tree."

We surrounded the Christmas tree as though our lives depended on it. We watched as a man wrapped string around the branches. Dad grabbed one end of the Christmas tree. The three of us grabbed on to branches. We were off, dragging our Christmas tree the short distance from the floral shop to our apartment. The four of us marched together as though we had just accomplished something special. With Dad leading the way, the base of the tree in his hands he led us to our apartment.

Dad led the way, up the stairs, through the hallway into our kitchen. Mom was waiting for us at the top of the stairs, telling us not to make so much noise. She told Dad to quiet down, and to be careful not to scrape against the walls as we dragged the Xmas tree through our hallway toward the kitchen window.

Mom opened the kitchen window to the fire escape. Dad pushed the Christmas tree through the opening. He climbed out and tied the tree to fire escape railings; making sure the winter winds wouldn't blow it off the fire escape. The Christmas tree would remain on the fire escape until Christmas Eve. As far as you could see, backyard fire escapes had Christmas trees tied down. They remained throughout rain, snow, and wind until the night before Christmas. Santa's helpers removed the trees to be decorated. Dad and Mom said so.

Every day, up through Christmas Eve, we peeked, checking and rechecking, making sure our Christmas tree was still attached to our fire escape. Snow fell throughout the days prior to Christmas, settling on our Christmas tree. Mom and Dad must have had a truce. They weren't fighting as often. We were asking if Santa was bringing presents for us. They said Santa was very busy. But, he would bring presents to good little boys and girls. It was a happy time.

Shortly before Christmas, I walked past the corner florist. I spotted Bob picking up Christmas trees and wreaths that had been knocked over by the wind. He told me the man in the floral shop told him he would pay him to pick up fallen Christmas trees and wreaths. The man paid Bob? Bob was six years old. He was being paid. I thought I'd help him. He made it clear…this was his gig, not mine. Geez!

Christmas Morning

Mom shook me awake. Penny jumped from our bed onto the floor, most likely heading to settle in under Dad and Mom's bed. I spotted Al and Bob, tearing into Christmas presents. Mom sat me under the Christmas tree near my presents. A manger with Joseph, Mary, baby Jesus complete with three wise men, camels, and sheep, watched over our presents.

Christmas tree branches held decorative glass tube candles. They lit up with bubbling colored water. Additionally, real candles were attached to branches. Colorful Christmas balls, all shapes and sizes mixed in with tinsel and long garlands intertwined throughout branches completed our Christmas tree. I was opening gifts; Dad caught my attention. He'd gotten up from where he was listening to Christmas music. He approached the Christmas tree. He lit a match and began lighting candles. Got the visual?

Something prompted me to walk into our kitchen, announcing "Mommy, Dad's lighting the candles."

Mom turned to me. "What did you say?" I repeated.

"Dad's lighting candles on the Christmas tree."

Mom's apron flew off as she passed me. Did her apron need to come off? Mom made a beeline into the living room, yelling, "Dominic, what are you doing? Are you crazy?"

Dad and Mom began blowing out lit candles. Dad said, "It's all right, Anna." I was watching them. Mom pulled Dad away from the Christmas tree as she snatched candles from branches, tossing them to the side. She was upset. Dad was trying to calm her down.

Mom collected the candles and headed for the kitchen, telling Dad, "I'm tossing them out." Dad followed her, mumbling. Eventually Dad returned to listening to Christmas music. I peeked at him – only to receive one of his laser looks. Come on. The apartment could have burned down. I was a hero?

Christmas Presents

Bob received a cowboy outfit. The outfit was complete; a shirt, pants, belt, two holsters with a pair of six shooters topped off with a cowboy hat. He put his cowboy outfit on, over his clothes. He wore his cowboy outfit throughout Christmas day.

He wanted to wear it outside. Mom said it was too cold. He persisted. He was allowed out if he stayed close to our apartment. Bob walked up and down our street, showing off his cowboy outfit. He returned to our apartment when he got cold or when Mom called him to come in. We were safe as long as Bob patrolled our Flatbush Avenue block.

Al received an erector set. Let me tell you! It didn't take long before he erected a Ferris wheel. A small motor turned the Ferris wheel round and round with little seats rocking back and forth were the finishing touches. Al showed an early interest in putting things together. Once after observing dad adjusting a loose doorknob, he decided to undo dad's handiwork. He undid the entire doorknob. The problem! He wasn't able to reconnect the pieces.

Dad arrived home to a gaping hole where the doorknob should have been. Upon further inspection he spotted the screwdriver, pliers, nuts, screws, and the doorknob on the floor near the door. Dad fixed the doorknob. I don't recall him saying anything to Al, not one frigging word. Now, if that had been me!

My Christmas gift was a copper sheet kit. It came with a burnishing tool; when heated and applied to copper sheets lines tracing designs animal figures appeared. Was I excited? A penknife would have made my day. What were Dad and Mom thinking?

Maybe they were attempting to figure out what interest – if any – I had that would keep me occupied. But, when I approached the wall socket to connect the burnishing tool, I was headed off by Mom. "Johnny, wait until Daddy helps you." That was as close as I got to using it. Thankfully, other toys were available. We received a miniature wooden bowling ball game. We set up the pins on our living room wood floor. Rolling wooden balls across a wooded floor, crashing into wooden pins throughout the day and, for the next few days, echoed throughout our apartment; and, I'm sure the apartment below us.

Singing Christmas Carols with Dad

Dad gathered us around him in the living room. He opened the daily newspaper to a page where Christmas carols were printed. Get the picture! No one, I mean absolutely no one, to my knowledge then or now in our family can carry a tune. What was Dad thinking? But hey, he was in a festive mood.

He encouraged us to sing along with him. I don't know what got into us. Maybe it was his voice. We got the giggles, big time. Poor Dad. He was trying his best. He was urging us to sing along with him. *Silent Night, Holy Night.* We had serious fits of the giggles. Mom was in the kitchen, preparing Christmas dinner. Occasionally she let out a laugh. Dad gave up. He disappeared into the kitchen. We retreated to bowling wooden balls over hardwood floors.

Mom prepared a super Italian Christmas supper, gravy, meatballs, and sausages with a side of fresh ricotta cheese for pasta. A fresh salad, followed with fresh fruit, completed Christmas supper. The smell of Italian gravy simmering for hours with ingredients of meatballs and sausage to be served with pasta, Italian bread, salad, and desserts of pastries.

That Christmas memory of opening presents and feasting on Mom's Italian Christmas meal remains with me to this day. Unbeknownst to Dad, Mom, Al, Bob, and me, nineteen forty-seven would be our last family Christmas together.

Every now and then throughout the years while enjoying the Holidays, my mind slips back to yesterdays with Mom in an apron, her beautiful long hair flowing down over her shoulders, in our kitchen, preparing an Italian meal, with garden herbs and fresh tomatoes in a simmering gravy filled with meatballs, sausage, and pork.

Mom welcoming us as we trekked in from playing or from school. Dad calling out to us from across the hallway between the apartment and our playroom. Visiting Santa Claus with Mom. Shopping with Dad for 'the perfect Christmas tree.' Bob picking up fallen Christmas trees and wreaths. Bob dressed out in a cowboy outfit, complete with hat and six shooters. Al constructing a Ferris wheel from his erector set; me staring at a burnishing tool kit along with outlined figures on cooper plates. A few memories among many others collected over the years. Thankfully, I'll always have them.

Penny's 'Not So' Christmas

We returned from visiting relatives. We followed behind Dad and Mom as they entered our apartment. Dad's voice was loud and clear. Our Christmas tree was lying down on the living room floor. It was surrounded with broken Christmas ornaments, silver tinsel, and light strings mixed in with our toys. Penny was lying within Christmas tree branches, staring back at with yellow wide-opened eyes. She was tangled with silver tinsel.

Dad went into action, He headed for Penny from the branches. Mom herded us away from the living room. Penny shot out from the branches, ducking from Dad as she raced for a hiding spot, most likely under their bed. She didn't make it.

Mom blocked her path, scooting her with flailing hands and arms away from their bedroom. Penny did an about face, hightailing it to the kitchen. A fatal mistake. Our kitchen was small. Dad cornered her. We watched as Dad, with Penny secured in his arms, headed for the door. Penny was never seen again. Hopefully she found a new home. Penny was a super cool cat.

Saint Jerome School
1944

We attended Saint Jerome Catholic School, just off Flatbush Avenue. We didn't qualify to ride the bus from our area. We walked several blocks to school, regardless of the weather.

I recall a heavy snowfall. We opened our apartment hallway door leading to the street. We were surrounded with snow piled so high; it was over our heads. A narrow path cleared by workers pointed the way to school.

"A snow day. No such luck." On snow days, we attended school; in our case, Al, Bob, and me walked through snow drifts to attend school. First graders like Bob were included. Ah…those days are gone. Today's kids would receive 'snow day' approved absences from school. Mom bundled us with heavy coats, pulled down hats covering our ears, and scarves wrapped around our necks. Mom pinned mittens to our sleeves with safety pins. God forbid we lost our mittens.

Returning home from school, Mom checked that everything we left with in the morning returned with us in the afternoon. "Get out of your coats, boys. Hang your wet mittens and scarves over the radiator. Put your socks and galoshes under the radiator to dry." We'd huddle close to the radiator to warm up. Our radiator looked like a colored rainbow.

Covering School Books

Hard covered books were required to have covers. Covers could be purchased at school. But, Dad elected to make covers for our schoolbooks from newspapers. He measured cutouts to fit tightly around them.

He sealed the newspaper with scotch tape. They stood out from others made from plain brown paper. Our covers even had incomplete cartoons, which kids commented on. The nuns didn't question my covered books wrapped in newspaper.

Newspaper came in handy for homemade kites. Dad laid out small pieces of wood for the frame on our living room floor. He fit newspaper to fit it over the wood frame. He secured the newspaper to the wood frame with scotch tape. String was attached to the wood frame. A tail was a string with little pieces of ribbons tied to it. We flew the kite in and around Flatbush vacant lots. Dad ran the kites into the air. Once the kite was flying, He let us hold on to the string. We watched the kite turning in all directions, high above us. It was fun.

School Lunch

Mom's Sandwiches

Mom prepared sandwiches on wonder bread. They were filled with tomatoes, lettuce and smothered with mayonnaise. They were wrapped in wax paper. Try swapping that out. The wax paper ensured the sandwich would be soggy by the time lunchtime rolled around. It didn't take long for kids to know about Mom's soggy sandwiches. Al, Bob, and I ate them whenever we weren't able to swap them out, one of Mom's soggy sandwiches. One swap-out did the trick! Their interest in swapping out lunches with me were over. New kids anxious to make friends were the best marks for swapping out.

The Zipper

Al recalled; a sister observed me exiting the bathroom with my pants zipper at half-mast. She told Al to tell me, "When he comes out of the bathroom, he needs to be zippered all the way up." Years later, recalling the instance, Al admitted he deliberately didn't tell me. Not his problem!

School Fight

A boy and I got into a verbal argument in the school playground. It led into pushing and shouting at each other. Boys and girls were gathering near us, attracted by our scuffling with each other.

We approached each other, he swung; I ducked and grabbed the sleeve of his jacket. It came off. I swung the jacket at him. The zipper crossed over his face causing a red welt on his cheek. Sisters alerted to yelling and shouting of boys and girls were on the scene. What do they see? Me swinging the jacket at the boy. We were led away to principal's office. The kid was crying. I was denying. He was comforted by Sisters. I on the other hand was led by a sister with a good solid grip on one of my ear lobes to the principal's office.

I tried explaining; he started the fight. He continued crying. We were told our parents were being contacted. My plea! Please do not contact Dad. We didn't have a phone. He was at work! Sisters reacted as though I wasn't there. Minutes passed.

A sister entered the office with the kid's mother. Sister Principal explained what occurred. The red mark on the kid's cheek was pointed out. I wasn't feeling confident. Mom arrived. Sister Principal introduced our mothers to each other as she explained what happened. Both mothers were upset. Both apologized to Sister Principal.

Mom apologized to the boy and his mother! She was holding the kid's hands, asking if he was OK. He whimpered, "Yes." What the hell! Sister Principal released us to our moms. No school that day.

Mom was upset. I told her, "He started it."

She responded, "Wait until your dad gets home." I went into begging mode. She held my hand very tight, pulling me as we fast-walked home. I went into overdrive, sniffling, telling Mom, "The other boy started it."

To top it off. I told Mom I had left my mushy sandwich on wonder bread filled with wet slices of tomato and lettuce in my desk slot. "I'm not making lunch for you again, Johnny." We continued fast walking. "I'm hungry, Mom."

She continued scolding me, "Don't you ever fight in school again."

I assured her I wouldn't. "Please don't tell Dad." Mom grew calmer as we walked. I was beginning to feel better. I continued pestering her, "Mom. I'm hungry."

Mom stopped short of a Woolworths store. "Listen to me, Johnny. You go into the store and take a seat at the counter. Order a hot dog and a soda. When you finish eating, tell the waitress you were hungry. That you have no money. Do not tell her where you live. You can cry, if that helps." I wasn't going to question Mom. Mom stopped a block from Woolworths. She'd wait there for me. 'Sounds like a plan!'

Lunch at Woolworths

I entered Woolworths. I walked straight to the counter and took a seat on the round stool. There was another man at the counter. He smiled at me. The waitress smiled at me – good signs. I ordered a hot dog and a soda from the waitress. She was young. She smiled, again, as she returned with my hot dog and soda. I wolfed down the hot dog and drank the soda. She asked if I wanted anything else. I knew better. She removed the dish and glass. She returned with a piece of paper with the amount written on it.

I looked down at the paper. I muttered. "I don't have money. I was hungry." The man looked up at the waitress, then at me. I didn't move. I stared down at the piece of paper. The waitress said nothing. The man said nothing. She removed the paper from the counter, putting it in her pocket. "Don't do this again. Go on. You need to leave." I spun off the stool and hurried through glass doors out into the street.

I spied Mom up the block waiting for me. She was smiling from ear to ear. She began laughing as I raced toward her. She pulled me alongside her. We walked home. She was hugging me. She looked back as we crossed the street. "Did you eat the hot dog?"

"Yes."

"Did you drink the soda?"

"Yes." Mom was laughing. We were both laughing. Mom was happy. Me too.

Mom never mentioned the incident at school to Dad. I didn't have to run for the springs. Aside from Mom being upset with me fighting and me being confused with everybody apologizing to each other, I enjoyed Mom's sending me to Woolworths. The incident was an all-time good moment with each other. Mom's smile and her laughing were priceless. A good day!

Sister Principal Meets Dad!

Another fight! Sister stepped out of the classroom to retrieve something; just enough time for us to horse around. A boy and I yelled at each other from across an aisle of desks. We tossed stuff at each other. It got out of hand. I chased after him in and out of chairs, desks, and aisles.

Boys and girls were up and moving toward the front of the class room; some were shouting "call Sister, call Sister!" Others were laughing and encouraging us. I lost my balance, grabbing a chair and releasing it as I turned a corner. The sound of the chair crashing into a glass bookcase registered with me. Broken glass scattered everywhere. Boys and girls were out of their seats, screaming, running toward the front of the classroom. Sister returned. Everyone talked at the same time. Fingers were pointed at me and the kid. Sisters arrived. They calmed everyone down. Girls were crying. Sisters took in the broken glass scattered throughout the room. I was in deep doo-doo.

Our class was removed. They were placed along the hallway walls. The boy and I pointed at each other. A sister took hold of our neck shirts. She marched us in tandem pass boys and girls lined up against hallway walls. Off to the Principals office, again! I was doomed. I immediately offered up Mom as my contact. I said Dad worked. Mom was home! She could contact her. I prayed they contacted Mom. They didn't.

Dad entered the office. He was dressed in a suit, shirt, and tie. His eyes took in the surroundings. He found me sitting on a bench a few feet away from the boy. I involuntarily looked up at Dad. I received 'the look.' I was dead meat. Sister Principal remained behind her desk. Introductions were made. Neither Dad nor the other parent, a woman, seemed comfortable. Brief nods were exchanged between them. They took seats in chairs next to us.

Sister Principal apologized to Dad and the boy's mother for summoning them to her office. She went into a description of what occurred in our classroom. Her voice was stern. She explained our involvement in a very serious fight, in our classroom. Based on reports from our classmates, she graphically described what happened. "Sister stepped out of the classroom for a moment. These boys misbehaved. They got up from their seats and chased after each other throughout the classroom. They knocked over chairs. They scared other children. They caused a chair to crash into a glass book cabinet."

At this point, the other boy shouted, more to his mother, "He made the chair hit the glass!" Sister continued. My memory of her description was pretty much on target. In fact, I couldn't add anything or explain it any better. But, we weren't provided opportunities to offer rebuttals. Duh!

We were guilty, pure and simple. Dad appeared calm. He asked a few questions. He looked at the boy, asking if he was OK. He apologized to the boy's mother. He apologized to Sister Principal. Does this sound familiar? I was close to peeing in my pants. Sister Principal advised both parents of their responsibilities to pay for the replacement of the broken glass in the book cabinet. They agreed. Everyone was nice. Not nice enough to exchange Christmas cards; nevertheless, nice.

Dad was calm throughout the entire explanation of what occurred in the classroom. Maybe things were going to be OK with Dad and me? Dad sneaked me 'the look.' Oops! Following a stern talk with both parents, Sister Principal dismissed the boy and his mother. She asked Dad to remain. Sister reminded him this was my second fight incident. A confused look from Dad. Apparently, Mom forgot to review her visit with Sister Principal. My stomach was filling with a sickening feeling. I had to pee. I asked to use the bathroom. A Sister escorted me.

Sister Principal related her meeting with Mom. She had a good memory. Dad was calm, respectful, even embarrassed. Once again, this time, with feelings, Dad apologized to Sister Principal. He assured her I'd receive a 'good talking to' and have 'playtime' taken away from me. Hey! A good talking to, my playtime taken away. I was OK with that. I knew better. I began positioning. I needed to get away from Dad. I raised my hand. "Sister, could I please return to my classroom?"

"No! You cannot return to your classroom."

Sister explained to Dad, another fighting incident would be very serious. I could be transferred out of the school. Again – Dad shot me a look. He assured Sister the fighting will stop. She looked at me. "Do you understand, John?"

I went into crying mode. "Yes, Sister." I knew if I was thrown out of the school, something really bad would happen! I didn't know what that would be. I just knew that I wasn't gonna let it happen.

Dad had his hand on my shoulder as we left Saint Jerome school. He kept it on my shoulder until we were out of sight from the school grounds. I didn't count the head slaps from Dad as we walked home. There were a lot. We passed people. They didn't bat an eye. In those years, when a kid misbehaved, it was accepted for parents to discipline their kids. Geez! Geez!

I managed to work out a plan, sort of. Nothing complex. Hey! I wasn't capable of coming up with complex plans. Dad loosened his grip from my shoulder. Now, mixed in with head slaps, he settled for an occasional shove forward. My only chance was to break for the stairs as soon as we entered our apartment building. I needed to get into our apartment, past Mom, on my way to the springs.

We reached our apartment. Dad reached for the door handle. As he opened the door. I broke away, flying up the stairs. "Where do you think you're going?" He shouted as he rushed after me. I flew into our apartment, passed a surprised Mom, on my way to the bedsprings. Dad entered the apartment, shouting "Anna, you didn't tell me he was in a fight at school?"

Mom countered with, "What are you doing home, Dominic?"

I made it to the springs, sliding and griping my fingers as tight as I could to the mattress springs. I heard Dad and Mom arguing. I'm sure Dad was pissed, not being told by Mom about her meeting with Sister Principal. I imagined; they both fetched the broomstick.

I had company, again. Penny and I made eye contact. Her yellow eyes staring, seemingly smiling at me. I stared back at her. Dad and Mom arrived. Dad with his weapon of choice, Mom's broomstick. Penny stretched out her front legs and yawned. She shot me a last look, before shooting out from under the bed, passing both Dad and Mom, on her way to a new hideout.

Dad probed, searching for a 'hit'. I held tightly to the springs. Dad moved the bed, I moved with the bed. I attempted to grab or swipe at the probing boom stick when it came close to me with a free hand. It was time to call Mom. Oh, wait, she was there already. Dad said, "I'm going to send you from here to Carnarsie." He bent down for a better look at where he needed to probe with the boom stick. I matched his moves with counter moves.

The threats and probing continued, interjected with hits and calls for Mom. Dad's tie swung loose each time he bent down for another round of peek-a-boo. Eventually, he was flat on his stomach staring at me. I stared back. I heard him say something to Mom. They both laughed. Dad retreated – just like that. He managed a few hits. I deserved them. I knew the drill. I remained under the bed until Mom came for me. God forbid I'd miss supper.

School

I didn't enjoy school. I was a daydreamer. My mind wandered. If daydreaming was a course, I would have passed with flying colors. If I sat near a window, I'd stare out at buildings, trees, clouds, people, pretty much anything that caught my attention.

Doodling

When confined to a desk, away from a window and being bored, I'd dip my ink pen into an ink well. I'd fill in as much of the white areas as I could to match the black areas. Very creative!

Arithmetic Tables

Arithmetic consisted of learning the tables. Adding, subtracting, multiplication, and division were drilled into us. It was memorization. I was good at memorizing. It got interesting when a boy or a girl was called to the black-board to work out a problem. All eyes were on them. If he/she had difficulty, hands waved for attention to be called on. When I knew an answer, I'd join the waving hands. It was fun.

Spelling

While I enjoyed reading, my spelling wasn't up to par. In spelling bees, Sister searched out kids who didn't raise their hands. I was a marked target. I hid behind boys, dropped pencils, bent down to avoid being called on. Sisters always found me. Hands were always waving to be called to spell a word correctly. Actually, there were times I was called to the blackboard, to record correctly spelled words. Where was spell check?

Ink Well Opportunities

Sometimes, I'd dig the point of my ink pen into the wood top of my desk, creating a small opening. I'd rip a small piece of paper and stuff it into the small opening. I'd dipped my ink pen into the ink well. I dipped ink into the small opening I made in my desk. So much for dentistry.

Catching a fly was challenging. Once caught, I removed its wings. I covered it with black ink from my ink well and watched as it wandered around my desk. There was a girl sitting in front of my desk. She was wearing a white blouse. I carefully placed the wingless inked fly on her shoulder. It wandered around her shoulder and back of her blouse. A trail of tiny ink covered fly-feet were visible on her blouse.

A kid sitting next to me spotted the walking fly recording tiny black fly feet on her blouse. He began to giggle. I shot him a look. He calmed down. I carefully flicked the fly off her shoulder. I wonder if her parents figured out what the little black spots on her white blouse were.

Altar Boy vs. Torch Boy

I was recruited to become an altar boy. Really! To begin with, I wasn't keen on remaining after school to study Latin or for that matter, anything. When Mom learned of my enrollment, she was pleased. I decided to give it a try. I was OK with memorizing the colors and names of vestments worn by priests. Studying Latin was my downfall. I managed memorizing a few verses before hitting the wall. Becoming an altar boy wasn't in the cards for me. Mom wasn't pleased.

Sisters agreed to enroll me into the Torch Boy program. Training as a torch boy, referred to as Torches. It wasn't near as challenging as training to be an altar boy. Latin wasn't required. Mom was placated.

Primary responsibilities for torches were to assist services at special Masses. Six torches were assigned to special Masses. Three to each side of the altar. We were briefed in proper spacing, knowing when to kneel, and to be mindful; that the large candles we carried were lit. Within a few short days, after completing a 'rigorous training' program I received my first assignment. It would be my one and only appearance as a torch boy.

Dressed in long white flowing robes made me feel important. We followed the priests and altar boys as they entered the altar area. We'd take positions opposite each other on the altar, three to a side, remaining silent, standing and staring across the altar at each other throughout the Mass service.

I was positioned to follow the first torch onto the altar. As he passed me, I blew out his candle. A spur of the moment reaction on my part. He had to continue past me, entering the altar area carrying an unlit torch. Not to be out done, the third behind me, leaned forward and blew my candle out just as I turned to enter the altar area. Now two of us were standing on in the altar area with unlit candles. The boy behind me had the only lit candle.

We stared across the altar at three torches holding lit torches. They stared back at us. There were smiles. Followed by a few giggles from students in the rows attending the Mass. Sisters noticed and were silencing boys with stern stares and whispered threats. The boy whose candle I blew out was choking on giggling. I manage to remain silent. Priests facing the sacristy, saying Mass in Latin, were unaware of the mini disruption behind them. The service continued without a hitch.

Following services was a different story. Six of us were separated into teams of three. The team of torches across from us received reprimands. Our group weren't as lucky. The sisters were very upset. Some expressed disappointment. Others were shocked. How could we be so disrespectful in church?

I apologized. We all apologized. The lead torch boy took the opportunity to say I blew out his candle first. That didn't sit well with the Sisters. They zeroed in on me and the boy following me, who blew out my candle. The first torch was reprimanded and excused. The two of us, who blew out the lit candles were released on the spot from the program. Sorry, Mom.

Playing Hooky

I played hooky, not often. I walked to school with Al and Bob. I separated from them, just before entering the school play area. I veered off, headed for a billboard about a block away from Saint Jerome school. I climbed a billboard to a flat area near the bottom of the sign. I sat there content, without a care in the world.

Sometimes, another kid climbed up. We'd count cars, watch construction workers, eat lunch, and talk about stuff. People passed below. Some looked up at us. We looked back at them. Some shouted for us to climb down. Mostly, we were left alone.

We listened for the school bell, announcing classes being released. We climbed down, joining boys and girls leaving for their homes. If I had money, I'd head over to the construction area. A lunch truck sold hot dogs and hero sandwiches. My favorite was a hot dog with red pepper and deli mustard, or I bought a hero stuffed with salami and peppers. I'd continue home, most likely playing in our playroom.

A Shortcut Home From School

Al and I decided to take a shortcut home through a vacant lot across from Saint Jerome School. We happened on a group of older boys. They were cooking spuds, 'potatoes' in an open fire. Cooking spuds wasn't unusual throughout vacant lots in Brooklyn. The spuds gave off a heavy thick burning odor as they roasted over an open fire pit.

We attempted to pass the group. An altercation with them ensued. I can't recall the particulars. A guy held Al. Another boy placed a charred end of a stick onto his opened palm. Al reacted, big time. He broke loose of the boys, running for all he was worth.

I watched Al running. I was grabbed as I attempted to chase after him. I struggled to break away. I tripped or was tripped into the fire where potato 'spuds' were cooking. My pants legs caught fire. The sight of my dancing trying to put out the fire on my pants legs was enough to scare the boys running away in all directions. I managed to beat out the fire.

Al was long gone. I was alone. I ran back to Saint Jerome school, straight for the church. Once inside, Sisters came to my aid. I don't recall much. I woke up. Whose face do I see? Dad's! He was staring down at me. I was in a place, maybe a hospital or an infirmary? I had burns on both of my shins. My right shin was burned more seriously than the other. My burns caused minor scars to my legs. Today, they're mostly gone.

Dad asked. "Who did it?" He wanted names. Did they attend my school? Why was I walking through the lots? "It's a shortcut. I don't know," I replied. I couldn't tell Dad anything about the boys. I didn't know them. I never mentioned Al was with me? Al recalls the incident. He never told Dad about it either. To this day, Dad never knew Al and I were together that day. Al's burned palms, my pants, and leg burns. No worries.

Kitchen Fire

Our stove was located a few inches from our kitchen window. Sometimes, when Mom was cooking, she'd prop the window open and tie the window curtains to one side away from the stove. Mom stepped away from the kitchen briefly. A gust of wind may have loosened the curtains, causing them to swing over the stove, catching fire. Bob was home. He spotted the fire. He ran down the stairs, out of our apartment into the street, yelling "Fire" to no one in particular. Bob pointed to our apartment and kept yelling fire. A man followed him into our apartment. He helped Mom put out the fire. We were lucky. Way to go, Bob.

Radiator Burst

Dad was at work. We were on the bed with Mom. It was a cold winter day. The sounds of stream and hot water running throughout radiators were welcomed. Suddenly, hot water and steam gushed out from the radiator. A steam-valve burst? Hot water blew directly into their clothes closet, which was constructed of cardboard. In no time, it was soaked through. Dad's suits and Mom's dresses were soaked through as well.

Mom moved us into the kitchen. She contacted the building superintendent. Shortly after, a large man in striped overalls and a big belly arrived at our apartment door. We remained in the kitchen until the 'super' repaired the radiator. The damage was complete. The cardboard closet and clothes were soaked through. Mom removed Dad's suits and jackets and her dresses. She hung them on the clothesline. It was good that Dad was working part time at a clothing store. He was able to replace some of their clothes.

An Unusual Supper

Dad was working his second job. Mom prepared an unusual supper. Al, Bob, and I were seated at the small table in our kitchen. Mom placed a box of cereal on the table. She filled our bowls with cereal and poured hot water into them. No milk. No bread. No dessert. Just cereal with hot water. We ate supper. That was it. I wonder what Mom ate. I wonder if Mom's ill? Or whatever it was developing into was beginning to affect her.

Neighborhood Butcher

A neighborhood butcher shop was a few store fronts from our apartment. Mom sometimes sent me to the butcher with a note for him. He was a large man. He wore a white apron, mostly covered with scraps and blood from the meats. He'd take the note and motion me aside where I waited while he finished serving customers.

Long, sticky brown-flypaper strips dangling from ceiling fans swung lazily above customers. No one paid attention to its passengers, dead and soon-to-be dead flys attempting to free themselves from the sticky flypaper.
I'd watch customers coming and leaving the butcher shop. Sometimes people smiled in my direction. Mostly, I'd busy myself drawing circles with my sneaker in sawdust which covered the floors.

Eventually, the butcher motioned me over to him. He'd hand me a brown paper bundle with soup bones for Mom. "OK kid, take this to your mom." That was it! I raced home, handing over the bundle of soup bones to Mom. She prepared delicious soup from the bones, sometimes bits of meat were attached to them. Dad spread globs of butter on Italian bread which he dipped into the soup. I wonder if Dad was aware of how Mom had gotten the soup bones.

The Heist

I was looking from Dad and Mom's bedroom window at people coming and leaving the A&P market across the street. Ladies were grocery shopping. Their grocery bags were filled with all types of food. Many gathered at the corner waiting on trolleys or buses to take them back to their neighborhoods.

I left our apartment, crossed Flatbush Avenue and took a spot near where the ladies came out of the A&P store, carrying their groceries. I watched for a long time. A lady emerged carrying two bags of groceries. She was heading for the trolley stop on the corner. I approached her, asking if I could carry one of the bags for her. She smiled as she handed me a bag.

I ran off with the bag of groceries. I ran as fast as I could, past where shoppers gathered for the trolley or buses. The lady cried out for me to stop. I kept running, rounding the corner, and holding tightly to the bag of groceries. I looked back. No one was coming after me! I ran, walked fast, trotted, and was breathing heavy. I circled several blocks, eventually ending up on the street behind our apartment building.

I was shaking. I was scared. I knew I had done something wrong. Eventually, I made the decision to make a break for our apartment, which was directly opposite the A&P store across from our apartment. As I approached the corner of our block. I kept an eye on the A&P store. I continued walking, hugging close to storefronts as I walked to our apartment. I didn't look back. I reached for the doorknob. I opened the door, flew up the stairs, into the safety of our apartment. Mom stared at me from the kitchen.

I was terrified. I never did anything like that. To this day, I can't explain why. I was beginning to calm down. Making it home without being caught was an adventure I'll never forget; but, one I'll always regret. I placed the bag on our small kitchen table. Mom looked at the bag of groceries, then back at me. "Johnny, where did you get this."

"I found it." I managed to say.

"Did you take this from someone?" I was frozen into silence.

"I'm sorry Mom." was all I could manage.

I watched as she unpacked the bag. She pulled out something wrapped in brown paper. She opened it, looked at me, rewrapped it, and placed it in our refrigerator. Mom put everything away. "Johnny, did you go to the A&P store?"

I replied "Yes."

"Johnny, don't you ever go near that store again. Do you hear me?" I heard her – loud and clear. I wouldn't be peeking through the Venetian blind window for a long time either. I avoided spending time in front of our apartment as much as I could. I didn't ride my scooter around our block for a long time. I grounded myself! Everything was off limits. Thankfully Mom didn't tell Dad. She never mentioned the incident to me ever again. On the other hand, it took me a while to get over it.

Happy Thanksgiving

Saint Jerome raffled off Thanksgiving turkeys. I don't recall the amount for each raffle ticket. I knew better then to ask Dad or Mom for money. A kid in my class won a Thanksgiving turkey. He was into trading baseball cards and comic books on Saturdays. I knew he wasn't good at flipping baseball cards. I caught up with him on the way home. I made a deal with him. I'd flip for the turkey baseball cards for him in exchange for the turkey. Flipping, matching baseball cards against the front or back of cards flipped by another player was a way to increase or lose baseball cards. I was a good flipper. I agreed to flip ten baseball cards for him, if he supplied the baseball cards. He agreed. I flipped and matched ten cards for him. He went away with twenty baseball cards. I came away with a Thanksgiving turkey.

I remember Mom's shocked look as I came into our kitchen with the turkey. "Johnny, what did you do now?" I explained what I did. Mom was smiling. She placed the turkey in our icebox.

I think we were invited to Aunt Mary's for Thanksgiving. We may have bought the turkey with us. I'm not sure Aunt Mary, as with most Italian families, began Thanksgiving celebration dinner with an Italian meal of tomato gravy, meatballs, sausage, pork, and homemade pasta. A Thanksgiving turkey along with traditional stuffing followed with many side dishes. Needless to say, everyone was stuffed. No pun intended.

Moms on a Mission

Mom heard an agency was conducting interviews for a commercial featuring kids. She dressed us. We were marched to a building somewhere in Brooklyn. We joined moms, boys, and girls in long lines. Mom filled out forms, answered questions from a lady before being directed into another room where other hopefuls were.

Mom was absolutely 'beyond nice' to everyone, with an emphasis toward men who sat behind tables assisting hopeful Moms with filling out applications. We were asked a few questions. There were smiles all around. We were told to turn this way and that way, asked to smile, to walk a few feet, to turn around for them, walk back.

Mom was super – smiling, encouraging us, and assisting in any way she could. Following the informal introductions, we were led into another room, joining up with other kids seated on benches with their mothers. Every once in a while, names were called out. Eventually, our name was called. We were ushered to another table where once again Mom was asked questions. The men met us with smiles, a few questions, and polite comments. We were motioned to another part of the room, joining a smaller group of Moms and kids. A lady would announce a name. My name was called. Mom was up. "Johnny, come on. They're calling us."

A smiling lady led me into another room. This time I was alone, facing men and women seated behind a long table. More smiles, a few questions, and people nodding among themselves at the table. I smiled. That's what Mom hammered into us. "Smile."

I was led back to the room where Mom, Al, and Bob were. Mom asked me what happened! "I don't know," I answered. Mom let it go for the time being. Bob's name was called. In a short time, he was led back to where Mom, Al, and I were seated. Al's name was called. He remained in that room longer than Bob and I. A lady came out of the room. She approached and introduced Mom to another lady who remained with us.

Mom was led into the room where Al was. Apparently, they were interested in Al. Al wasn't selected. Why? Al wouldn't smile. Mom was beside herself. "Al, all you had to do was smile and talk to the man." Mom was in a foul mood all the way home. Al didn't feel like smiling. Al could've been the next Clark Gable. We could have lived on his financial coattails. Thanks, Al.

Roy Rogers, Dale Evans, and Trigger

Roy Rogers, Dale Evans, and Trigger were touring the New York boroughs. Roy Rogers in person! Wow! What else was there! A large van approached the large parking lot of Macy's in downtown Brooklyn.

It was a moment I wouldn't forget. Trigger was being led down a ramp. The only horses I've seen were pulling peddlers carts. They seemed old and tired; worn out by years of pulling heavy carts loaded with fruit, ice, and coal throughout the streets of Brooklyn.

Trigger and a handler reached the bottom of the ramp. The sight of Trigger was electrifying. Hundreds of kids, yelling and cheering, welcomed Trigger. Trigger was huge! His blond mane and his tail were braided with colorful ribbons. We cheered and cheered for Trigger. He knew who he was. Once settled he stepped lively toward a circled ring. He raised his large head up and down and from side to side. He was acknowledging boys and girls cheering from behind roped off barriers.

Roy Rogers and Dale Evans appeared out of nowhere. Cheers from boys and girls announced their arrival even louder than they did for Trigger. Roy

Rogers and Dale Evans walked hand in hand, smiling and waving to kids as they walked toward the circle where Trigger was waiting for them.

Dale Evans was dressed in a brown cowgirl outfit. She wore boots and a brown cowboy hat. Roy Rogers was the first real live cowboy I ever saw in person. I'd wouldn't be far off if the overwhelming majority of boys and girls were seeing their first real cowboy and cowgirl in Brooklyn, N.Y. Roy Rogers' cowboy outfit was colorful. His sleeves had tassels hanging from them. He wore a large white hat. Six shooters hung from both sides of his belt. Cowboy boots with shining spurs completed his outfit.

Mom worked us up close to the roped off area. Roy Rogers and Dale Evans were working their way to where we were standing. They were laughing, shaking hands, and waving to the crowd. Bob and I were standing to the side of Mom and Al who were positioned to shake their hands with Roy Rogers and Dale Evans.

Sure enough, Roy Rogers and Dale Evans were right in front of Mom and Al. Roy Rogers extended his hand out to Al. What does Al do? He just stood there with his hands at his side. Mom urged Al to shake Roy Roger's hand. He stood there. Roy Rogers smiled as he continued down the line.

Mom went nuts. She was beside herself. Mom pulled us back away from the crowd, she was muttering to herself. She asked Al. "Why didn't you shake Roy Rogers' hand?" Al replied his favorite cowboy was The Lone Ranger. To my knowledge The Lone Ranger never visited Brooklyn. "Hi-ho Silver, away."

Dad and Mom Dancing with Al – Really!

Dad and Mom wanted to attend a dance hall. They loved to dance. They met each other at a dance hall. Al recalls Dad and Mom wanted to take him to a dance hall with them. Al nixed the offer. Hey! Al wouldn't smile for the advertising guys. He wouldn't shake Roy Rogers' hand. That should have given Dad and Mom a clear picture of Al's early profile. Our seemingly gentle brother could be as stubborn as a mule.

A Rose for Mom

One day while walking home from school, having nothing to do, I stopped into an alleyway where I had good luck in locating scraps on previous searches. I met an old man who tended a small garden off the rear of the alleyway. Sometimes, he put scraps aside for me.

On this visit, my search for scraps came up empty. As I was leaving, he called out to me. He picked a large red rose from the rose brush. He gave it to me for Mom. As soon as I entered our apartment, I handed the rose to her. She smiled as she took that rose, bent down, and hugged me.

Another time after fighting and being on the losing end, I stopped off at the alleyway, looking for the old man. He was sitting in his usual spot near his garden. He shook his head and laughed when I told him I lost a fight.

He wet and rolled a newspaper into a tight roll, like a tootsie roll. He placed the roll into my palms. I made a fist around the wet paper. He explained, the wet paper tightly wound into my hands would make my punches really hard. Unfortunately I never had time to tell a boy before a fight, hey, give me a minute will ya? I need to get some newspaper, wet it, and then we can have at it. Love that old man!

Al's Peanut Adventure

Our babysitter Deloris, took us to Prospect Park. Al ate peanuts – lots of peanuts. We were riding the trolley car from the park, the peanuts caught up with Al. An awful stench invaded the Trolley car. People looked in our direction. Deloris looked at Al. We all looked at Al. He crapped in his pants. Deloris moved us to the rear of the trolley car.

Al didn't smile, didn't say anything, just stared straight ahead. He never said a word. He just sat in his crap all the way to our Flatbush Avenue stop. Deloris told Mom what had happened. Mom was upset and embarrassed. She apologized to Deloris over and over. Mom steered Al to the bathtub. She stripped him of his pants and underwear and off he went into the bathtub which was filling with water, soon to be tainted brown. Mom was muttering to herself as Al was in a world of poop.

Impetigo!

Not a good thing! We managed to be infected with it. We must have been quite a sight. The three of us with scabs in and around our mouths and noses. Dad and Mom didn't notice it. Hello! The sisters did! We were sent home with a note written to Dad and Mom from them.

Mom didn't say much. We retreated to our playroom. Dad arrived home from work. We knew enough not to greet him, not this time anyway. When Mom gave him the letter from the sisters. Al recalls Dad becoming agitated, producing a heated discussion between him and Mom. We had impetigo. What! No hugs?

After supper, Mom bundled us up. Dad walked us up a few blocks to the doctor's office which was a few blocks away. He was upset. I didn't want to be blamed for us contracting impetigo! My antenna was on high alert. I took up a position behind Bob who walked behind Al, who walked behind Dad, like ducks in a row following their leader. Dad, with his head down, hands in his overcoat pockets walked like a man on a mission.

Tar Beach
The Rooftop

Spring and summer months were enjoyable times; many months spent relaxing on our apartment roof aka Tar Beach. We climbed a ladder to reach the roof. Once on top, a panoramic view of our neighborhood served as our family outing. We enjoyed the sun. Dad laid a huge blanket on top of the tar.

Blankets stuck to the tar, remaining throughout the summer months. Dad had a secret hiding place on the roof for storing the blanket throughout the winter months, whenever he could separate it from the tar paper. Climbing up to the tar roof wasn't fun for any of us. We climbed a ladder which was extended over open space, extending from our second floor level to the bottom ground floor. Al recalls not looking forward to climbing it.

Climbing that ladder introduced me to my gonads. When I stepped away from the floor, onto the first step of the extended ladder, I was literally dangling, frozen stiff against the ladder, eyes shut closed. "Don't look down, Johnny" – Dad's encouraging words. "Keep climbing." Looking down was the problem. The ladder with me on it, dangled about 40 feet of open space between me and the bottom landing below ours.

Coming down from Tar Beach rooftop wasn't a treat either. Dad growing impatient, bellowing, "Keep coming down, Johnny." As for Al and Bob, I have no clue of them climbing down the ladder. I remember Dad's encouraging words. "Don't look down, Johnny." That was my problem, looking down. I'd managed to get a foot on the first or second rung of the ladder, before freezing in position. My legs wouldn't cooperate.

Eventually, Mom's calming voice replaced Dad's frustrated pleas. She had already climbed down. Mom climbed back up a few steps on the ladder and took hold of my ankles, and gently guided me down me down the remaining steps. "You're almost there Johnny." Being near her was reassuring. A wonderful memory.

Saturday Chores

Saturday mornings began with Mom's list of chores for me and my brothers. I was assigned cleaning the bathroom. Mom filled a bucket with hot water. She added a rag and a bar of brown soap to the water. I wasted no time cleaning the bathroom. I cleaned the toilet first, to get it out of the way. I cleaned the inside, under the rim, both sides of the seat and the base.

I cleaned the tub, sink and washed the floor. Mom inspected the cleaned areas. I stood near her, holding a wet cloth in my hand to re-clean any areas – on the spot. I was anxious to get on with my playtime, exploring the neighborhood with friends.

Years later, in military boot camp, I was selected as 'Latrine Queen' of our barracks. I was responsible to supervise the cleaning of toilets, sinks, and floors. Our latrine competed against other barracks in 'white glove inspections' conducted by drill sergeants. I was destined for management.

Following Saturday chores, I looked forward to scouting out the neighborhood. The day was filled with boyhood activities throughout our streets. Trading baseball cards, comic books, chestnut string challenges, and penknife tossing contests. I made the round trading comics and baseball cards. I flipped for baseball cards if there was a card I needed.

Marbles was a popular game. Boys placed marbles into the center of the circle in the dirt. A larger marble was used by boys known as shooters. Using one hand, a shooter released the larger marble into the gathered, hitting as many marbles as possible out of the circle.

Saturday Night's Baths

Dad prepared our weekly baths. We shared the same bathtub water. He tested the water, tossed in a large bar of brown soap. Ivory soap wasn't a priority in our household. Mom used brown soap for washing dishes, doing laundry; actually, for all household chores.

Following Al wasn't as bad as Bob following me into the tub. It wasn't that Al didn't get dirty. He did but not as much as I did. I played hard throughout the week. Al got into the tub. Bob and I stood watching the color of the water turning into a light brown color. Not too bad! Al soaped up. Dad, using a pot from Mom's kitchen poured water over his head, completely rinsing him before Al stepped out of the tub. As Dad dried him off, I replaced him in the tub.

I stepped into the tub. I located the brown soap and soaped up. The light brown water quickly turned into a darker colored water. The large bar of brown soap laid on the bottom of the tub, it was difficult to see it under the brown water. Relocating it was up to Bob. Dad poured brown water over my head and body. I stepped out of the tub. Bob, stepped into the tub. His weekly contribution of dirt and grime was added to ours. Ugh! Bob got the short end of the stick. In thinking back to those baths, Bob would have been better off not bathing. Dad used one towel to dry us off. Once dried off, we got into pajamas.

Gotta Go

I was running home from a few blocks away. I was close to peeing my pants. I flew up the stairs, through the doorway, and into the bathroom. Mom was toweling off. She looked down at me. I stared up at her. Mom smiled. I wet my pants. Geez!

Penny vs. Resident Mice

Our apartment had resident mice. A favorite hiding area for them was in the bottom of cabinets under our kitchen sink along with stored pots and pans. Penny, our resident cat, knew the mice were hiding among the pots and pans. She patiently positioned herself close to the cabinets. Mom knew the mice often hid among her pots and pans. She armed herself with a wooden spoon which she banged against the cabinet doors before opening them.

Penny lined up just behind Mom. She was posed, ready to pounce on a mouse. Mom opened the cabinet doors. A mouse, alerted by Mom's banging on the cabinets sprang out. Low and behold, all hell broke loose.

Penny sprang into action. Mom swung her wooded spoon in the direction of the fleeing mouse. "The damn mouse is loose again. It's out!" cried Mom to no one in particular. Penny went into chase mode. The mouse went into escape mode. I wasn't any help. I just watched. The race was on. Another scream from Mom. "Get the mouse. Penny, get the damn mouse." Mom screamed as the mouse raced past her with Penny close behind.

More times than not, the mouse found a small opening or was able to run out of the apartment through the open door of our apartment. This time, Penny did catch the mouse. She took it with her under their bed; her favorite hiding place and, mine, when I was being punished. Penny had her way with the mouse.

Dad arrived home to shouts from Mom. "Dominic, that mouse is under our bed." Using Mom's broom, Dad used the wide end of the broom, trying to sweep both Penny and the mouse out from under their bed. Dad's curses had absolutely no effect on Penny.

I imagine Penny was amused. Eventually she scooted out from hiding, without the mouse. More cursing and muttering from Dad! He retrieved the dead mouse by its tail and flushed it down the toilet. Penny no doubt, proud of herself, eventually retreated back to her favorite area under Dad and Mom's bed.

Sure enough, another mouse would replace the previous one. It drove Dad and Mom crazy. Sometimes Dad emptied out the cabinet of pots and pans one at a time, hoping to catch a mouse hiding in one of them. Mom washed them before returning them to the cabinet.

Another time, while using the toilet, I spied a mouse hiding under our bathtub. I don't know how long it was there or how it got there. I stared at the mouse. It stared back at me, its black eyes not moving. It didn't seem concerned. I left it alone. I have no idea where it went.

Money Opportunities

Work always attracted me. I worked for a scrap man. I searched Brooklyn alleyways for newspapers, magazines, and wire hangers, earning a few nickels and dimes. I pulled loose change from sewers using a long round dowel with chewing gum stuck to one end of the dowel. I bartered for comics and baseball cards. Having change in my pocket made me feel good. It meant I could attend Saturday movies, buy candy, ice cream, comic books, and baseball cards.

Sometimes I searched through Dad's suit pockets for loose change. Most times I came across Juicy Fruit chewing gum, matches, and Camel cigarettes. The gum and cigarettes were useful in trading. When I did come across loose change, I was careful to remove very few, most times, none. I didn't want to get caught.

I did remove a cigarette or two from Dad's cigarette pack. I was careful to advance remaining cigarettes to the opened end of the pack. I wonder if he thought he might be smoking too much? I did the same with Juicy Fruit Gum. The cigarettes and gum were easy to exchange for a few pennies or even a nickel. Dad never missed the cigarettes or Juicy Fruit gum.

Dipping for Coins

Adults, mostly men waiting for transportation usually balanced loose change in one hand, a cigarette in the other. Occasionally, they dropped change into an open sewer. Retrieving coins from the bottom of sewers required a long wooden dowel, and chewing gum. Chewing gum was attached to the end of the dowel. The gummed end of the dowel was passed through the sewer grading, to the bottom of the sewer where the loose change lay.

We lowered the stick through the grading, with the gummed end of the dowel face down toward the coins. Timing was very important for a number of reasons. We waited until the adults were picked up. We'd rush in as fast as possible, before another line formed. When passengers shooed us away. We'd leave in search of another corner with an open sewer.

We had to race to school or become tardy when dipping for coins. When arrived tardy, we knew we avoided an absence report. Being tardy didn't cause parents to be notified. With two or three absences, a parent would be notified. Inclement weather, especially winter months produced the most coins; thanks to cold hands or bulky gloves. Older boys were our main concern. They knew where to find us. They didn't bother dipping for coins. They elected to lie in wait for us as we returned to school with collected coins.

At times when we were chased after by older boys, we'd split up, taking off in different directions. Shouting as we passed people. "The boys are chasing us." Most times, the chase ended with adults yelling for the boys to leave us alone. While dipping for change paid off, searching for scraps was safer.

Either way, I usually had money for Saturday matinees. Especially, if I worked for the scrap man. When I didn't have money. I'd hit the streets, trading comic books or flipping baseball cards to earn enough for the matinee. Growing up in the streets of Brooklyn provided me with an appreciation in bartering and positioning.

Saturday Activities

Kids weren't the only ones benefiting from Saturdays. I'd be safe in assuming parents throughout Brooklyn neighborhoods looked forward to their time alone on Saturdays. Dads and Moms had quiet time to themselves. Grocery shopping, repairing something, or listening to the radio, featuring Frank Sinatra, Bing Crosby, Peggy Lee, and Frankie Lane, along with big band sounds of Benny Goodman, Tommy Dorsey, Arty Shaw, and Les Brown to name a few. It offered them an opportunity to bang their brains out. Sorry – couldn't resist it.

Throughout spring and summer months families gathered on fire escapes hosting small gatherings with picnics. Voices speaking in broken English and in Italian echoed throughout backyards. Radios broadcasted baseball games. Adults cheered for The Brooklyn Dodgers, The New York Yankees, and The Giants. Boys were introduced to their Dad's favorite teams.

Parents listened to favorite radio programs featuring 'The Green Hornet' and 'The Fat Man' mixed in with musical and Italian programs featuring soap operas. Life was simple. Dad and Mom both spoke Italian. They spoke Italian in our presence when they didn't want us to know what they were saying. I was able to pick up 'street Italian.' But, you didn't dare let your parents hear you speak those words.

Continuing Saturday's Activities

Collecting baseball cards and comic books were popular and loads of fun. Saturday mornings found kids pulling wagons loaded with baseball cards and comic books. Some kids had their own spots on a block. I didn't have a specific place to hawk my baseball cards and comic books. I walked throughout blocks talking sports, trading baseball cards or comic books with neighborhood kids.

Saturdays were so special. No school, just neighborhood kids coming together to trade, barter and sell from their collections regarding baseball and comic book values. It was a comfortable introduction to positioning. Part of growing up. Flipping and matching exactly in the order of flipped heads or tails of baseball cards determined winners and losers.

Many a collection was wiped out in this fashion. Kids excelling at matching cards flipped for themselves as well as for kids they flipped for. Any winnings would be split. Losing would be the risk taken by the kid putting up the baseball cards. I was a good flipper. You had to be careful who you flipped for. Losing valuable cards had its Some kids purchased baseball cards. If they weren't serious collectors or flippers, they arranged for kids to flip for them.

Flipping Baseball Cards

A kid would flip as many heads up or tail backs of baseball cards as possible. Another kid could challenge the flipped baseball cards. Matching heads or tails had to be in perfect order. The pressure was on challenger. Not an easy as it may sound. Matching or not managing flipped baseball card/cards determined the winner.

Broken Nose

I got into a fight. I got beat. In fact, the boy broke my nose. I returned to our apartment, bloodied. Mom spotted me as I headed for the bathroom. "Show Dad what you did," or something like that.

Dad was reading a newspaper. He looked up from his chair. "Johnny, your nose is broken. Come here." As I got close to Dad, he pulled me close to him. He held me tight and twisted my nose back into place, 'sort of.' I backed away, crying. I think my eyeballs swapped sockets. Talk about pain!

Dad wasn't satisfied. He told me to find the boy and fight him again. Was he crazy? One beating was enough for me. Getting my butt kicked twice in one day! I don't think so. I left our apartment and slowly opened the door opening to the street. I peeked out, looking in all directions, hoping not to see the boy. Thankfully, he wasn't around. I reentered our apartment, standing just inside the door at the bottom of the stairs. After a while, I ventured quietly upstairs, settling into our boy cave.

A Few Good Years Were Coming to an End

More and more, we were becoming aware of Dad and Mom's arguing. When they did argue in our presence, it created a silence. Something wasn't right. I was confused. What's new.

A pattern formed. Mom attended Bingo. At least that was what we were told. Years later, we learned they were attending counseling relating to their arguing. Still later, they were attending psychological counseling. On nights, when Dad worked at his second job, we gathered around Mom in the living room after supper. She was calm and quiet; occasionally humming along with a song playing on the radio.

Mom crocheted doilies. She filled brown paper bags to the brim with completed round doilies. A friend delivered the bags to the factory. She returned with yarn and bags for Mom to fill. Mom earned money based on the amount of doilies crocheted.

When Mom wasn't crocheting, she busied herself washing and ironing clothes. She darned socks, wrapping them around a small piece of wood, shaped like a light bulb. Her eyesight was poor. She'd ask one of us to thread the needle for her.

More and more, when Dad and Mom were home together, they would get into heated arguments. We'd retreat to our playroom. If we remained in the living room, hearing them argue caused us to cry; causing them to stop arguing.

Sometimes, they both cried. Dad tossed up his cookies. They made up, only to go at it again, sometimes within minutes of crying. Once, Dad and Mom were arguing standing close to each other. Mom pushed Dad up against the wall. She held him up by his shirt, nearly off the floor. She was cursing. She was out of control. Dad didn't struggle. He kept his hands down. He pleaded with her to stop. Dad waited her out. It scared us.

It's difficult to put my finger on when Dad and Mom's arguing caught our attention. It just appeared. In retrospect, whatever was causing them to argue may have been festering for months. At any rate, we were witnesses more and more as their arguments took place in our presence.

We were witnessing a failing marriage. The growing arguments between them factored into positioning our futures. As time passed, it was obvious whatever the problem was, it wasn't going away any time soon. Even when

Dad tried walking away from arguing with Mom, she continued arguing. He would retreat to the kitchen. She followed him. The kitchen was where almost all their arguing took place.

Sometimes, Dad retreated to our living room where we were playing. Mom would hesitate arguing with him in our presence. Dad and Mom's agitation and constant arguing included us. How could it not? We weren't aware of anything specific, other than they argued with each other a lot.

Babysitters

With Mom or Dad not home in evenings, aunts or a babysitter watched over us. Much of it remains a blur. We were fed supper. They monitored homework assignments and read to us. Al always did his homework. Bob had none. He was in pre-school? Me. I either didn't have homework or I had reading assignments. As it was, spending time in school was challenging enough. Bringing homework home didn't make sense.

Reading stories after we washed up and ready for bed was the best part of the night. We were asleep before Dad arrived home. We hardly saw him. Mom's absence was not discussed with us by any of our aunts. It was as though Mom never existed.

Dad must have convinced our relatives that we were too young to understand about Mom's illness. How could they not be aware that Mom was transferred from our apartment to Bellevue Hospital's facility for the mentally ill? The day 'The men in White' took Mom away marked the end of 'a few good years.' Mom was gone. Dad didn't bother explaining why; not then, not ever; nothing!

A day at Rye Beach
Al, Mom, Bob, and John

Bob, John at Reese Park Beach with Mom
Mom was drop dead gorgeous

Dad and Mom
Brooklyn Apartment
1946

**Bob was born in WASHINGTON DC
1941**

John 1942
Washington DC

Aunt Billy with John
Washington DC

John, Al, and Bob
Al wouldn't share his candy with us

Dad and Mom
Al, still holding onto his candy
Washington DC

Mom and Al

Mom, Dad, Al, Bob, and John

Dad, John, and Al
1940s – Brooklyn

Celebrating!
Al, Mom, Dad,
John saluting, and Bob

John
Brooklyn

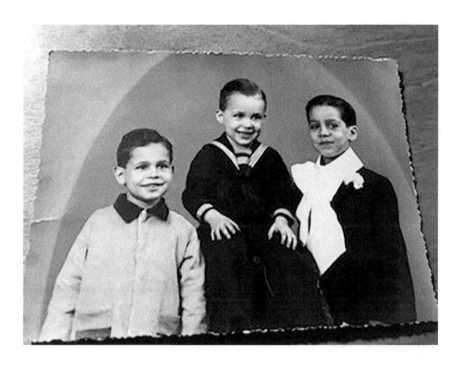

John, Bob, and Al
Al's Holy Communion

Mom and Grandma
Christmas – 1946

John, Bob, Al, Mom, and Dad
Our last family Christmas together
1946

Mom, Dad, and Grandma
Christmas 1946

Dad and Mom – happier days

Dad

Dad, Mom, and Bob
Washington DC

Aunt Rea, Mom, Uncle Tom,
Al, John, and Bob

Bob, John, Mom, and Al

Mom – early years

Mom (Anna Rose)
Teenager

Dad
Late 1930s

Dad and Mom
Love Birds
Late 1930s

Photos of Dad and Mom were difficult to locate. These few are the only ones available to me! Dad was five years older than Mom. They met at a dance hall; which were popular throughout Brooklyn, Manhattan, and the Bronx. Subway lines between boroughs connected to ethnic neighborhoods of Irish, Jewish, and Italian families. Based on where Dad and Mom's parents lived, it's a good bet they met in a Brooklyn dance hall.

Dad was a sharp dresser, good-looking, and a good dancer. Mom was young and 'drop dead gorgeous.' Dad was in a world of his own, self-confident, intelligent, and successful. Mom and Dad fell for each other's profiles. He was self-assured, confident, and cocky. He served in the army. Mom was several years younger. She was smitten by him. His strengths were Mom's weaknesses.

Dad's Profile
He had the Gift

Dad was popular. It didn't matter if he was entertaining Brooklyn buddies or working with fellow employees. He led the pack. He attracted attention. His mannerisms reflected a street profile. 'In charge, restive, competitive, and a braggart.' His Brooklyn buddies had nicknames. Little Red, Tony Boy, Buddy, and Rusty to name a few. Dad's nickname reflected his dark complexion. He was called Ace, as in, the ace of spades.

His mannerisms when dealing with co-workers reflected an opposite profile. He was measured, friendly, persuasive, and authoritative. He assumed leadership. In my opinion, he was the brightest guy in both groups.

Tony Milano aka, 'Tony Boy,' was Dad's closest friend. They roamed Brooklyn's neighborhood haunts as youngsters. They played cards in the back of Italian clubs. They served in the military. Weekends found them socializing at local dance halls where, incidentally, they met their future wives.

One thing separated them. Tony had an edge to him. He was street smart, and quick to defend an argument. Tony didn't talk much. Then again, he didn't need to. Dad, on the other hand, was a smooth talker. The two of them were a match for each other.

Dad and Tony Milano
Brooklyn buddies

Leaving Flatbush

Dad announced to us we're moving to Grandpa and Grandma's apartment. As always, it was out of the blue; Dad's preferred way of communicating. We gathered our toys, comic books, and baseball cards into a cardboard box. He set the box against our playroom door to keep it opened while we cleared the room out. As I carried my scooter out of the playroom. I told Dad not to forget our box filled with comic books and baseball cards. He answered. "Don't worry about that. I'll get it later."

I exited our apartment. A friend of Dad's called out. "Hey kid, put the scooter in the trunk." My scooter made it. Our comic books, baseball cards, and a few toys didn't make the trip. Geez!

What was going on? We were leaving our neighborhood. Everything I associated with. My friendships, Saturday matinee movies, venturing throughout neighborhoods, trading comic books and baseball cards. Earning a few nickels and dimes riding with the scrap man; being dropped me off in front of alleyways, hunting for wire coat hangers, newspapers, and iron scraps.

Sunday mornings with Dad and my brothers at the playground where hitting, catching, and chasing after baseballs were gone. My garden of string beans grown for Mom was gone. Sunday Italian meals with family members were gone. Sunday walks down Flatbush Avenue with Dad, Mom, Al, and Bob were gone.

The Bazooka Gum man standing on a street corner, surrounded with boys, attempting to blow the largest bubble and receive a free Bazooka Gum t-shirt was gone. Dipping for change from sewers was gone. Our boy cave was gone! Al, rising from our toy chest, scaring the be-jiggers out of us was gone. 'A Few Good Years' were gone!

Bob's Car Sick – 'Again'

We headed out on Flatbush Avenue. I noticed one of my friends. Our eyes met. We waved to each other. Flatbush Avenue became a memory. Bob didn't do well in cars. Back in the day cars weren't equipped with air conditioning. Dad and the friend were smoking. The car windows were closed. Cigarette smoke was circulating throughout the car. Chances were good that Bob was gonna be hurling. This was Bob's cue. He began hiccupping. Get the picture?

Bob leaned forward; choked and hurled. I hurled. Dad's friend yelled. "Hold it." a few times as he pulled the car over. Dad leaped out of his seat. He pulled us out of the rear of the car as fast as he could. We stood outside the car, wiping ourselves with rags. Dad gave us Juicy Fruit chewing gum. That did the trick. We never saw Dad's friend again. Ya think.

Grandpa and Grandma

Grandpa and Grandma couldn't have been warmer. We were greeted with open arms, hugging, kissing, and pinches on our cheeks. Grandma had a smile that made me feel good. Grandpa had a large mustache. He rubbed his big mustache against our faces when he hugged us.

Our move from our apartment on Flatbush Avenue to live with Grandpa and Grandma in their apartment located on 242 East 6th street was a surprise for us. Their apartment was smaller than our apartment on Flatbush Avenue. But it was longer, shaped like a subway car. A small kitchen, two bedrooms, and a small living room overlooking Sixth Street. Grandpa and Grandma raised six boys in this apartment? Hard to believe!

The bathroom was the size of a coat closet. It housed a toilet, a stand-up shower stall, filled with mops, pails, and detergents. A single light bulb hung from a wire from the ceiling. There wasn't a sink. There wasn't a bathtub. We were saved. Uncle Frank and Aunt Mary lived a few stoops down from them. There bathroom came with a bath tub. We bathed at their apartment on Saturday nights.

Sleeping Assignments

Al and Bob slept in a rear room of Grandpa and Grandma's apartment. I slept with a cousin, Jimmy, who lived with his parents, Jimmy and Lena next to Grandpa and Grandma's apartment. Each night I walked across the hall to their apartment to bunk with their son, Jimmy.

I was unsettled, to say the least. Bottom line; I wet the bed. I didn't say anything in the morning. I was on my way out the door when, Lena stopped me. "Johnny. Did you have an accident?" I did. Jimmy was off the hook. A rubber sheet was added to Jimmy's bed. It was the last time I wet a bed. I settled down. Lena fed me breakfast; cereal with blueberries. On Saturday mornings I watched T.V. in their apartment.

Grandpa and Grandma's neighborhood didn't compare to our Flatbush Avenue neighborhood. Our neighborhood was busy with activities. Grocery stores, playgrounds, movie theaters, and easy transportation were close by.

Within a few weeks we adapted to adjustments in our new surroundings. I had my scooter. I settled for riding back and forth on Sixth Street, using Grandpa's stoop as my parking spot. A treat was walking down third avenue to Entenmanns' bakery, to buy Grandpa's favorite 'day old lemon meringue pie for a dime.'

Shoe Box

Fifth Avenue was a few blocks away from Grandpa's apartment. Boys set up their shoeboxes close by bus, trolley cars, and subway stations. I mentioned it to Grandpa. He made me a shoeshine box. He loaded it with polishes, brushes, and cloths. Once again, I was on my way to earn money, maybe even more than I earned with the scrap man?

I carried my shoebox to the avenue. Boys stared me away from their corners. I walked further up the avenue. Sure enough I spotted an empty corner. I set up my shoebox business. I wasn't bothered by anyone. It wasn't long before I realized there wasn't a bus or trolley stop or subway entrance on my corner.

After a few days, I managed to talk a boy into letting me shine shoes with him. He was doing a brisk business. He let me work alongside him. Customers still waited for him to be available. Shining shoes wasn't going to work out for me.

I swapped out my shoe box with him. I sold him my supplies for about thirty-five cents. I told Grandpa what I did. He didn't say much. He took the shoebox. I'm not sure what he did with it. He was disappointed. He let me keep the money.

Thanks to Dad, I didn't have to be concerned with trading comics and baseball cards. They remained in a cardboard box carton, holding open the door to our playroom? It took me a while to get over it. Saturday matinees were available with Aunt Mary gathering us together with cousin Angela, her daughter, to see a movie. Cowboy movies were replaced with Bambi, Snow White, and Uncle Ramos. It was OK. Aunt Mary and Uncle Frank were good to us.

Meeting Dad's family was interesting. With the exception of Angela, our first cousin, other cousins weren't born yet. Sadly, we missed out on events, holidays, and growing up together. It was worst with cousins on Mom's side of her family. Once Dad moved us out of our apartment on Flatbush Avenue, we lost contact with them. It would be years before we reestablished ties.

Sunday dinners at Grandpa and Grandma's included uncles and aunts. Grandma's Italian meals, prepared over a wood burning stove were delicious. Pasta, meatballs, pork, and beef were served along with a salad. Grandma was a wonderful cook, as were all our aunts. Sunday gatherings at both Grandparents families, remain treasured moments.

At Grandpa and Grandma's

Al, Bob, Angela, and I sat at a small table. Grownups ate, talked, drank homemade wine and laughed. Grandpa made sure we had a very small amount of Benedictine. Grandpa was cool.

Mom's name was never spoken in our presence. One exception! It involved Grandma and me. In 'broken English' she told me, "Sometimes your Mama came to visit us."

Just to be clear. I missed Mom's smile; her voice greeting us as we walked into our apartment. "Boys, wash your hands." On cold snowy days she made us place wet gloves, hats, and scarves over a steaming radiator to dry. Rubber galoshes were placed on newspaper close to the bottom of the radiator. Mostly, I missed Mom because she was always around to make me feel her warmth and her love. Go figure!

With Mom gone, Dad working, it fell to Grandpa and Grandma waking us, feeding us breakfast, and sending off to school. In retrospect, it was a lot to ask our grandparents to monitor us. Dad wasn't his old self. He was edgy.

He had a lot on his mind, duh. He'd check with Grandpa and Grandma, asking if we did our homework. I wasn't concerned about bringing home homework. He was upset with me for forgetting to bring home homework. I pleaded; I completed homework in class. From time to time, I bought home a book to read. That seemed to satisfy him. Grandpa and Grandma never pressed me to show them home work, I'd wave a book in their direction as I headed to the back room.

Mostly, after spending a few minutes in the back room, I wandered outside to play. Stoopball was fun. Swimming in the Carnarsie River with kids from the neighborhood in warm weather and wandering throughout the neighborhood whenever I could. Dad was nowhere to be found. He was working. Mom was confined to a mental facility. Grandpa and Grandma were in their apartment, hoping we were behaving ourselves.

Roof Climber

For no reason other than joining boys already sitting on the edge of a roof; I climbed up to join them. The building was small. It was a garage for small trucks. The roof wasn't very high. We were sitting on the edge of the roof with our legs hanging off it. Kids yelled to me, "Your dad's coming." Sure enough, Dad was walking toward us. With my legs dangled over the edge of the roof, I didn't have time to hide. It was too late. Dad looked up. He spotted me. I managed. "Hi, Dad." We shared a moment staring at each other.

Dad was wearing his Army reserve uniform. He didn't yell. He told me and the kids to climb down from the roof. Once we were on the ground, Dad told us climbing the roof was dangerous. He sent the kids home. He was nice. "It's time for dinner, Johnny." My sixth sense told me I was in a jam. I ran ahead of him toward our apartment, which was a half block from the building. I zipped up the stairs, washed up, and sat down to dinner with my brothers and grandparents. We were settling in while Grandma served soup.

Dad came up behind me. He introduced my face into Grandma's hot soup. I sobbed. Dad pushed my head into the soup dish a second time, for good measure, I guess. Good thing we didn't have a dunking stool. Dad overplayed his hand.

Grandpa stood up from his chair. Big mistake! Grandpa walked to Dad, shouting in Italian. He stood up close to Dad. Dad backed off. He was silent. He didn't say a word to Grandpa. He calmed down. He took a seat near Grandma. Grandpa continued scolding him. Dad left the table. He lost his temper in front of Grandpa and Grandma. Grandpa's reaction got Dad's attention.

Dad was dealing with difficult times. All of us were. He was under pressure. His decision with Mom had to weigh on him. Then again, how could we know what he was dealing with? Grandma wiped my face with a cloth. I sobbed throughout supper. I joined Al and Bob in the back room where they were watching T.V. Dad came into the room which was his usual pattern when saying good night to us. "Johnny, stop crying." He shoved a few pennies in my hand as he offered me advice. "Don't climb the roofs. You could get hurt." Really?

Afterschool Treats

On weekdays after school, Grandma always had snacks for us. Monday snacks leftovers from Sunday's meal, mostly meatballs and macaroni refried in oil, were given to us. Most times there wasn't enough for the three of us. Al received Sunday's leftovers. Bob and I ate cold cut sandwiches. Afterwards, we were able to play outside. Grandpa's stoop was our official meeting place for neighborhood kids. We played 'stoop ball,' 'kick the can,' and spin the bottle, my favorite.

A Dirty River

Directly across the street from our apartment was a free-flowing river. The water wasn't deep. Sometimes, the slow-moving river carried 'stuff' down river. The river was the top of his list of no-nos. It's cargo of pollutants flowed toward a clothing manufacturing factory on the corner of Sixth Street. On hot summer days, without a care in the world or for the pollutants flowing in the river, we cooled off in the river. A story circulated, a boy dived into the river. His head was wedged in the opening of a large discarded milk container. We were careful not to jump near where the kid stuck in the milk container was. Duh!

I was drying off when a kid limped out of the water. He could hardly stand. His ankle hit something hard when he jumped in the river. The milk container? Just saying. I half-carried him to his stoop. Kids ran ahead, alerting his mom. She was waiting on their stoop when we arrived. She grabbed his ear. As she dragged him by his ear, she thanked me. He was doomed. To the kids, I was a hero. Dad would have been proud of me! 'Johnny? What were you doing in the river?' No way was I going to tell him. Why invite another round of 'a face in soup!'

YMCA

Big Red

Summer times, I was allowed to swim with friends at the YMCA. The YMCA was free. We swam in the YMCA pool. A marked improvement over the river. Swimming in the YCMA pool was skinny-dipping. No problem. We stripped down. We jumped into the pool. A few boys already in the water told us to keep an eye out for Big Red. Sure enough, "Here comes Big Red." He was fat. A large man with receding red hair. Big red was friendly. Ya think! He liked to grab kids, hug 'em close before tossing them in the air, catching them as they reentered the water. We avoided Big Red. Hello.

Summer evening attracted adults to Stickball games, played between cars. Dad played. Uncle Frank umpired. Men smoked and drank beer. Kids watched the games and ran after balls hit out of bounds. Women leaned out open windows yelling at kids.

Street Fight

Once while sitting on our stoop I spotted a crowd of people gathered around two men fighting near Uncle Frank's apartment. I walked to Uncle Frank's stoop. The men fighting were stripped bare to their waist. One held what looked like a stickball bat. The other held a short stick with a chain dangling from it. When they occasionally struck each other, blood would flow, causing outcries from onlookers.

The men backed off from each other before circling again for another strike against each other. Sometimes standing, staring at each other, holding weapons by their sides, not advancing, seemingly hoping the fight was over. Eventually, men stepped in, separating the bloody, exhausted, and, probably, thankful fighters for ending the fight.

Man Who Lugs Lumber!

A strange man often walked through sixth street. He always carried a two by four wooden piece of lumber on his shoulder. One time we were gathered around Grandpa's stoop. The man was walking toward us. We knew he was someone to avoid. A few kids started to laugh at him as he drew closer to us. A girl said something to him. He turned and walked toward her. Kids scattered. I don't know why I didn't. I stayed near the girl on the stoop. He approached her. He was muttering. That should have been my cue.

I stupidly took a position, standing in front of the girl. No problem. He turned his attention to me. I caught the flash of the two-by-four piece of lumber swinging in my direction. I turned away. I was hit squarely in my back. I blanked out. Kids alerted Grandpa. I ended up sitting in a chair in Grandpa's kitchen. After a while I was allowed to return to the stoop. Dad came home. I held my breath. They didn't tell him what happened. Whew!

Saint Thomas Aquinas

The weeks of summer passed. We were enrolled in Saint Thomas Aquinas. Dad gave Al and me briefcases. Al used his briefcase for school books. I used my briefcase for snacks and comic books. We settled into school, new friends and routines. The differences between Saint Jerome and Saint Thomas Aquinas weren't many with one exception.

It was Easter season. A sister who taught music was leading us through Easter songs. "Here comes Peter Cotton Tail." Kids were assigned to taping banners on walls throughout the classroom. I noticed a girl and a boy standing together on a chair. They were taping an Easter banner to the wall.

Sister was playing songs on the piano. She wasn't paying attention to the kids standing close together on a chair. The boy was dry humping the girl. "Dry humping in third grade! Wow!" Sister played the piano, leading our class in singing Easter songs. A few giggles from kids confirmed my observations. Singing and humping continued.

Sports

Racing Activities

Students from neighboring schools were invited to participate in a race track team. Our school held tryouts. I qualified for the track team. We'd race against other schools. The tournament was held in Red-Hook; a tough neighborhood. Once there, we competed in preliminary races. I won in my group; qualifying me to represent our school. Cool!

I joined other kids in the warm up area. A kid came to me. "Hey, you running in the first race?"

I responded, "Yeah."

He pointed out a kid, standing with a group of kids. "You better stay behind him."

I answered, "Why?"

"Just do it." Again, I asked him why did I have to stay behind him.

"Just do it." as he walked away. The kid who I was supposed to stay behind in the race was staring at me. His friends were shooting me unfriendly looks.

We lined up a few lanes apart from each other. The starter gun went off. The kid was fast off the starting line. But, he wasn't faster than me. I caught up to him, making sure I didn't pass him. A kid passed us like we were standing still. I couldn't catch the kid who passed us. But, I knew I could pass the kid I was told not to pass. I didn't give it another thought. I passed him, finishing in second place.

I received a medal. Sisters were pleased. We headed for our school bus. I wanted to get on that bus as fast as I could. I mixed in with my school group, looking over my shoulder to see if any kids were following me. We boarded our bus. It was the first and only event I competed in while enrolled at Saint Thomas Aquinas. I wasn't thinking if I would race against the kid again.

The Final Move

People began visiting Grandpa's apartment a few times, at night time. They spoke with Dad. On one visit, they were introduced to us. Dad told us they were from the special school. Actually, they were representatives from Catholic Charities. They smiled and asked a few questions. That was it. We were excused to the rear room. After they left, Dad met with us in the back room. He told us we were being transferred to a special school. We would be there for three weeks. Bob remembers, it was for a few days, not three weeks. Whatever! We were on the move again. In less than two months, following Mom's transfer to a mental facility, Dad arranged for us to be transferred to a 'Special School'; not really. We were on our way to an orphanage. Little by little, I noted changes in Dad. In retrospect he was dealing with challenges he couldn't have been prepared for. No doubt about that. He was unable to bring us into the loop. It could have made a difference in the long run. Dad's decisions affecting Mom and us were damaging to us. Particularly for Mom; I shudder at what her first days, nights, and weeks were like. It had to be a hellish nightmare for her.

Dad and Rosalie?

Rosalie was a niece of Mom. Their mothers were sisters. For whatever reason known only to Dad, she accompanied him on the day we were removed from school.

A week or so after the visit from Catholic charities representatives, we were removed from our classrooms by sisters. We were taken to the Principal's office. What did I do now? I entered the office. I spotted Al and Bob sitting on a bench. Dad and Rosalie sat on chairs in front of a large desk. What the hell? Alarms set off. Here we go again! What was happening? Where were we going this time? 'A special school!' Really! We were being transferred to the special school. That had to be it. We sat in silence.

Sisters followed us carrying files, missed homework assignments. What was happening? Dad certainly knew what was happening. We didn't know jack s--t. Occasionally, Rosalie smiled in our direction. Dad didn't look at us. He was all business. He and the principal talked awhile. Minutes passed. Dad, Rosalie, and the principal stood up from their chairs. Goodbyes were exchanged. Nothing was said to us. We didn't ask questions. "Why start now!" When Mom was with us, we would have. Mom's disappearance, unexplained moves, zero explanations from Dad and, now, another adventure! We were being introduced to a new phase in our lives.

The Red-Brick Building

We walked out of the school. It was cloudy and overcast with light rain falling. Dad said nothing, Nada! We walked slightly behind Dad as was the norm. It was a short walk. We arrived at a Red-Brick Building. Funny, I recall seeing the red-brick building a block or two before reaching it; not realizing it was our destination. We were leaving Grandpa and Grandma's apartment the same way we left our Flatbush apartment. No notice. Thanks, Dad.

A sister met us at the entrance. She led Dad and Rosalie away from us. Several sisters appeared. They were smiling. They led us to a room where we sat on wooden benches. The room was dimly lit. Planters overflowing with ferns were lined along one wall. Ferns can grow anywhere! As sisters came and went. They smiled. It was reassuring.

We were taken to another room. This one was better lit. The walls were covered with photos and paintings of the Holy family and Patron Saints. In the center of one wall was a large picture of Jesus, crucified on the cross. Small lit candles were placed on a table at the foot of the picture.

It was quiet, and scary. We didn't speak. We waited for the next interruption in our lives. Finally sisters entered the room. They motioned for Al and me to follow them. Another sister entered the room. We were taken to separate rooms. I was asked a few questions. I arrived back before Al. Bob was crying. He was left in the room alone while Al and I were undergoing a Catholic interrogation. Bob didn't have a clue what was happening. He was six months shy of his sixth birthday! What the hell was Dad thinking?

Missed Clues!

We might have figured something was up when we were questioned by the folks from The Catholic Charities Organization. Coupled with the morning of our last day, Grandpa hugged us many times before sending us off to school. Grandma gave us brown paper bags, filled with candy.

Everyone but us, it seems, knew what was ahead for us. Then again, Dad wasn't around that morning. That was normal. He left from wherever he spent the night. We walked the few blocks to Saint Thomas Aquinas school as though everything was OK. Little did we realize we were attending our last day of school. It would be months before we saw Grandpa and Grandma, uncles and aunts again.

Goodbyes

Saying goodbye: No hugs. No advice. Nothing! Dad and Rosalie walked out of that building on that September morning in 1947. We were officially signed into an orphanage. Yippy! OK! Fair enough. Do I get to keep my scooter? Or would it be left behind like our comic books and baseball cards when we left our Flatbush apartment? At any rate, we were on our way to a special school, our third home in less than two and a half months.

Uncles and Aunts

It's worth mentioning here. Were our uncles and aunts aware of Dad placing us in an orphanage? Years later we were told several of them tried convincing him to let us live with them, reasoning it would serve to hold our family together, until he was able to work through his difficulties. Call it headstrong – whatever. Dad refused. His mind was made up. Unfortunately, his decision played into severe repercussions in later years for him and us.

Chapter Two
Mount Loretto

Not so Good Years

Mr. Butler, Aka Mr. B

Dad was gone! We're sitting on a bench in a semi dark room. A sister sat with us. The door opened. A man entered and stood a few feet from us. He held a hat in his hands. He was tall, thin, and looked unfriendly. His nose stuck out from his thin face. It looked like a hook. His small eyes searched ours. He and Sister exchanged a few words. She introduced him, "This is Mr. B." He didn't smile. He hardly looked at us. He seemed to be in a hurry. It was for sure, he wasn't related to any of our families. Sister walked us to Mr. B.'s car. She smiled, turned, and walked back inside the Red-Brick Building. It was just Mr. B and us.

Where was Dad? Where was anybody? His car side doors were covered with wood paneling. It was the first time I saw that type of car. To this day, when I see a photo of a 1948 era Woody, my mind goes back to the day we rode in one.

Mr. B. didn't speak. When he did speak, he told us where we were being taken to a school? Here we go again. Three young brothers, being moved again, within two and a half months after Mom was removed from our apartment; and us. Mr. B. told us to sit together in the rear seat of the station wagon. We began talking among ourselves, just nervous kid talk. Mr. B. got into the car, turned to us, and told us to be quiet. We did just that. We rode in silence, three boys sitting in a large car.

It was a short ride. We stopped at the end of a long line of cars. Mr. B. told us we were taking a ride on a Ferryboat. We were on our way to Staten Island. Was the special school there? We were clueless. It was our first ride on a ferryboat. Mr. B. followed the car in front of us, onto the ferry. He parked

109

behind a car. The ferryboat sounded a horn. We were on our way. I looked out the rear window trying to see the water.

A long lineup of cars were in front, in back, and alongside of our car. They blocked my view. Mr. B. stepped out of the car. A silly hat floated to the side of his head. His overcoat was buttoned all the way up to his chin. He remained close to the front door of the car. He had us roll down the windows. The fresh smell of the sea mixed in with cigarette smoke and exhaust pipes entered the car.

Mr. B. was smoking a cigarette. Every once in a while he'd look toward us through an open window. People were standing near their cars, talking, smoking, and taking in the view. He didn't let us out of the car. I guess he was afraid of us trying to escape or something stupid like that. Yeah, sure! The ferry ride from Brooklyn to Staten Island could have been more exciting. Being restricted to the car prevented us from enjoying the surrounding sights in the distance.

Little by little thoughts fell into place. Mom was gone. Aunts and uncles were gone. Cousins were gone. Friends were gone. Sisters in St. Thomas Aquinas were gone. Grandparents were gone. Dad was gone.

Exhaust fumes mixed with cigarette smoke created a perfect setting for Bob to begin hiccupping, a sure sign of what was to follow. Mr. B. wasn't aware of Bob's carsickness. A huge eruption, hurling chucks of whatever was in Bob's stomach out of his stomach. He hurled up and over the front seat where Mr. B. sat. It took a second or two for us to follow Bob's lead.

Whatever we had eaten came out as though it had a life of its own. We joined Bob in hurling. We hurled on ourselves. We hurled over the front seat. We were hurling, big time! Mr. B. looked toward the hurling noises. I looked up at him. He seemed to freeze. His eyes were very wide. The cigarette dropped from his lips. He yanked the door open, yelling for us to get out of the car. Sure! Now, he lets us out! Vomit covered the back seat, the floor and driver's side on the front seat.

We had to be quite a sight standing alongside the car, crying, with vomit on our faces and hands and clothing. Mr. B. attempted to calm us down. People gathered around the commotion. They passed Mr. B. newspapers, probably,

The Daily News or the Post. He gave them to us to wipe ourselves off. People continued passing us newspapers and an occasional rag to wipe ourselves.

Mr. B. was leaning into the driver's side. He wiped off his seat. Once in a while, his head reappeared backwards, trying to catch fresh air. We continued crying, wiping vomit from our faces, arms, and our clothes. Mr. B. was wiping out vomit from his car seat with one hand, and the other holding a handkerchief to his face. He emerged from the car. He headed for the nearest railing, and hurled into the sea. He bent over, holding on to the railing with both hands hurling. Could this day get any worse?

The ferry docked. We emerged with the odor of vomit accompanying us. The car stunk. We all stunk. Mr. B. drove to a gas station. Once again we were told to remain in the car while he went into the gas station. Thankfully the windows were open wide. He returned with wet paper towels and a pail of water. He cleaned himself and wiped off his seat. We got out of the car. He handed us wet paper towels to wipe down our seat and ourselves as best we could. Surprise! He gave us chewing gum. I bet he carried chewing gum with him on future runs.

We settled down for the remaining ride to our special school with windows half-way down. We weren't clear of the odor. But, it was as good as it would get. Nothing looked like 'Brooklyn.' I noticed many woody areas and homes spaced out nicely. Everything seemed to be open areas, filled with trees and green grass. It was as though we entered into another world! Where were we? The only green areas I was familiar with were in Prospect Park.

Mr. B. remained silent throughout the remaining ride. He smoked and he coughed. My guess is he was pissed. Hey! Bob started it. We must have been quite a sight. Not to mention the foul odor in the car even with the windows rolled partially down.

Father Drumgoole
Mount Loretto, aka The Mount

Mount Loretto was founded in the 1890s by an Irish catholic priest, Fr. Drumgoole. He arranged for 194 acres of prime land on Staten Island, just across from Manhattan, New York, to be designated as an orphanage – housing – for boys and girls.

Fr. Drumgoole named the Orphanage 'Mount Loretto' for the sisters of Saint Francis, assigned to the orphanage. Eventually, over years, in line with the numbers of boys and girls being admitted, Priests, brothers, counselors, and lay-persons joined the sisters at The Mount.

The Mount was our special school. Dad made it appear to be a special place just for us. What could I possibly accomplish in a special school in three weeks? Three weeks grew into eight and a half years. OK; my response remains the same. Oops! Maybe that's what Dad meant. Or maybe he felt we'd fall in love with the place? What the hell. We'd get over it. *Really?*

Arrival at The Mount

We were passing a large hill on both sides of the road when Mr. B. slowed the car down. He turned into a road which seemed to pop up all of a sudden. He continued following the road passing kids playing in an open field. I was excited to see kids playing. I think I was trying to feel it was going to be OK. We passed pass the cottages on the right and cornfields on the left. I was engrossed watching kids playing when the car came to a stop alongside a large building. I wondered what was waiting for us.

We piled out of the station wagon. We arrived. Mr. B. headed toward the porch which fronted the entrance of the building. A few sisters came down the porch steps toward us. They were smiling. A welcomed contrast from 'Mr. B's personality.' Sisters were dressed in the traditional black. A thick black belt surrounded their waist. Rosary beads and a thin white corded rope with three separated notches hung from her black belts. Their faces reflected a freshness. Starched white linen surrounded their faces.

We had to be a sight. Our clothes were stained with vomit. Our hair and our skin were stained with vomit. The stench had to be overpowering. Sister took in the sight before her. Mr. B. was animated, swinging his hands back and forth. He was look in our direction, pointing us out to the Sister. We looked back at them. Sister was nodding to Mr. B., glancing in our direction, taking it all in.

Mr. B. disappeared into the building. We never saw him again. Sister turned her attention to us. We stood side by side, taking the fresh air. Holding her smile, Sister marched us forward, up the porch stairs, into a large open area. Everything was painted white. The walls, ceilings, doors, window trim…everything was white. More Sisters appeared. Their voices sounded happy, matching their smiles. They were our first bits of joy, considering how our day was shaping up; beginning with Dad plucking us from classrooms, dropping us off in the red brick building before disappearing.

113

We were taken to another room, stripped of our clothes, placed in separate bathtubs filled with warm, soapy water. We washed from head to toe with white soap. Mom always used brown soap. Bathing in separate bathtubs was a first. After drying off we changed into clothing different from the ones we arrived in. Sisters told us our cloths would be shared with other boys. Hopefully the smell of vomit would be gone. Our special school was taking shape.

Within the first hours of arrival to our 'special school,' we were cleaned and dressed in jeans and flannel shirts along with pull over sweaters. Nothing matched. We were walking rainbows. The days passed smoothly. Sisters were wonderful. They explained, we were quarantined for a few days to make certain we were healthy before joining other kids. OK. No problem.

We ate together in a small dining room. We were the only kids in the building. Al swears there were girls in the infirmary. He heard their voices! Maybe they were in another part of the building? Bob and I never heard the girls. The food was good; not homemade Italian meals but it was good. A treat was occasional ice cream. Mr. B. was gone. The sisters were kind. I began to relax.

The previous months began to take its toll on us. Particularly with Bob. He was just five and a half years old. I cannot imagine what he was feeling. Bob was OK when we were together. We had to rely on each other. We passed the time with board games, watching kids playing, being examined by doctors, and assisting sisters with cleaning chores.

We cleaned the floors by placing rags a few feet in front of us, take a running start, fall onto the rags, hitting our butts, and sliding down hallways. It was fun! Sisters kept us occupied with stories, answering questions, always smiling and being nice. We continued watching kids playing from the building's windows. I looked for boys riding bicycles or scooters. There were none.

We pestered the sisters. "When are we going to be able to play with the other boys?" We were told, it would be in a few days. We didn't realize it, but, our days in quarantine was as good as it would be for many years.

Sisters in White

On the second or third day we were taken into a part of the building we hadn't seen before. This room was white. White cabinets, white walls, white chairs, and white tables; off to an open room were beds with, you guessed it, white railings. Sisters were dressed in white met us as we entered into the white room. Up to this point we were exposed to sisters dressed in traditional black. These Sisters were nice. They explained we were in the infirmary. The beds were for boys who became sick, just like a hospital. The white beds were empty.

We were seated on a bench. A white chair and table was positioned in front of the bench. We were quiet. The only movement was Sisters chatting among themselves; and on occasion, smiling at us. We were used to Sisters smiling; they always smiled. I sensed a difference. Did it have anything to do with 'The Men in White?'

I was directed to sit in a chair a few feet in front of the bench where we were seating. Sisters appeared on both sides. They were speaking to me nonstop as they rested my arms firmly on each arm of the chair. A rubber tube was wrapped around my upper arm. It felt tight. I felt my shoulders being held tightly by a Sister. I looked in the direction of a tray, next to my chair. The tray had cotton balls, a needle, and glass vials. The needle really registered with me.

A Sister was speaking to me as she applied pressure against my arm. I spied the needle. This was my clue. I yelled, really loud. Sisters joined voices in attempting to calm me down. I watched red blood filling a vial. It was all the encouragement I needed to continue crying. It was over. I was taken to the bench, sniffling and looking at the white bandage on my arm. Sisters continued comforting me.

Bob was next. He imitated me, crying as soon as Sisters led him to the chair. (No pun intended.) He was loud. He continued crying throughout the procedure. Al was next. He settled into the chair. Sisters were speaking with him. He never uttered one freaking word throughout the procedure. What the hell? Very disappointing!

That was the worst part of being quarantined. That night we were served ice cream. It was a high price to pay. The next day had us back to polishing hallways on rags and, staring from windows at kids playing on the playgrounds.

Sisters explained that kids marching to and from the dining hall were organized by age groups, assigned to cottages numbered from 1st to sixth cottage. Older kids assigned to the sixth cottage were followed by age groups from the fifth, fourth, third, second, and first cottages. Kids in the sixth cottage were transferred to the 'big side' when they reached the age of thirteen. It didn't mean anything to me. Dad told us we were to be in our special school for three weeks. I was looking forward to returning to Grandpa and Grandma's apartment.

Sisters continued briefing us on what to expect once transferred to our assigned cottages. The sisters administering to us while in quarantine hold a special place in my heart. They were kind and welcoming. Well, maybe not the sisters in white.

Father Kenny

Three kids from each cottage arrived at the quarantine building. They were our escorts. We were taken to the sixth cottage where Father Kenny lived on the second floor of the cottage. We stood at an opened door. Our escorts stood behind us. I noticed the long line of beds down the length of the cottage. They were two to a side, separated by an aisle. All the beds were made up. The bed were framed in iron railings, painted in white. Could the sisters in white be far behind?

Father Kenny was an Irishman who happened to be a priest with a reassuring smile. His eyes were large, deep, and dark blue. His voice was warm. He addressed each of us by our first names. An opened carton of Kool cigarettes laid among piles of papers on his desk. He must have read my mind.

He explained how we would be separated into age groups. He smiled, taking it nice and easy, smoking, talking, and putting us at ease. I had a feeling; He had done this before! He told us we'd see each other because our cottages were side by side. He went on to speak about the cottages, counselors, and recreation activities. In the interim, three boys, each from a cottage assigned to us, appeared at Father Kenny's door. We were introduced to them.

A boy assigned to me had a smile that out-smiled everyone else. His face was filled with freckles. He was short and chubby. Froggy was his name. He wore enormous eyeglasses with a frame, covering half his face. The glasses made his eyes pop out. He had thick red hair. It flowed in all directions, even down over his ears.

I was released into his care. Froggy laughed a lot. He introduced me to every boy we passed or bumped into on our way to my new home; fifth cottage. It seemed everybody knew Froggy. Froggy and I hit it off pretty good.

All cottages were designed alike on the outside and inside. Box numbers were written on the wall over each box where a kid sat. Hinged lids on boxes enabled items to be stored. Cottages included play areas, bathrooms, showers, and wash areas. Cottages held sixty kids assigned to box numbers.

Each cottage was staffed with a Sister. They over looked housekeeping, cleaning chores, laundry needs as well as mending clothes in a small room equipped with a sewing machine. Counselors over looked discipline behavior. The fifth cottage housed a small candy store used for kids to purchase a few candy items. Our cottage sister operated the store twice weekly.

Cold weather or severe summer heat forced everyone indoors. Play areas had board games, Chinese checkers, Ping Pong paddles, and even comic books for kids to check out when confined indoor. In good weather, cottages emptied out. The gymnasium had eight half-court basketball courts for team and individual pickup games and team practices. Boxing and dodge ball shared space as needed.

Fifth cottage was sandwiched between Al's sixth and Bob's third cottages. Age groupings in cottages played a major role in us not remaining in close contact with each other; which remained throughout our time in The Mount.

Mr. O'Connor Aka Mr. O.

Once transferred to the fifth cottage, I took in my new surroundings. Kids playing board games, ping pong, and a few peering over shoulders of kids reading comic books. I was taking it all in when, out of the blue, a hush silenced talking, laughing, and playing.

A deep voice rang throughout the cottage. "Everyone to your boxes." I looked toward where the voice came from. A tall man standing inside the doorway entrance was taking in the movement of kids hurrying to their assigned boxes. The voice belonged to Mr. O., my fifth cottage counselor.

He was standing ramrod straight. His eyes found me. It was easy. I was the only kid standing in the middle of the hall. I didn't know where or what to do "John, you're assigned to seat box number 29. It's alongside that wall, in the rear, under the window. Go to your box now." He pointed me toward the direction of my box. I spotted the number 29 written on the wall directly over my box. A kid smiled at me as I approached my box. I sat down.

Mr. O. was imposing; At least, to me. He was tall with closely cropped white hair resembling jumbled wire. His facial features were long, with cheekbones ready to pop out from his face. His eyes were buried deep, into his forehead. His voice was deep. It carried through the entire cottage as if he was standing directly in front of you. It was scary. I adjusted my behavior.

In those first days, Froggy pointed out Jr. Counselors. They were older boys, assigned to watch us when Mr. O. was otherwise involved. Froggy pointed out which ones to avoid. All the more reason to hang close to Froggy in those first days on the small side. In time, I began mingling with other boys.

I was invited into their activities, ping-pong, checkers, and outdoor games. It wasn't long before I understood the layout of my new surroundings.

The gymnasium became my hangout. I watched the games. In time, I joined in half-court basketball games. I shot foul ball from the line, underhanded. Dodge ball, indoor sprint races, and boxing lessons pretty much filled the indoor activities. In time, new friends, sports, and separate cottages played a role in forming separations between me and my brothers. When Dad began visiting us, weeks after we arrived, we were able to develop a routine. We gathered when Dad scheduled a visit. Following his departure, we went our separate ways.

An early memory involved Bob and another boy fighting. I was hanging out with boys in the large play area, located directly across from all the cottages. On any given day, it hosted hundreds of boys – all ages playing stickball, baseball, roller skating, tag games, you name it! Hundreds of kids roughly managing to play games associated within their age groups, rarely interfering with each other.

I was in the playing area when I spotted Froggy running toward me. He shouted "Your brother is in a fight!" I followed down the slope, toward a group of boys surrounding them. Bob and the other boy were lying on the ground side by side kicking and punching at each other. I threw a kick at the other boy. He rolled away from Bob. They were both on their feet. The boy came at me. Bob was running.

I pushed him to the ground. I kicked him a few times before a Jr. Counselor pulled me off him. Boys backed off, disappearing into the play areas. I was facing a Jr. Counselor. He wasn't smiling. Instinctively, I pushed back. That did it! I was hauled into fifth cottage. He introduced me to 'campus.' Campus was punishment assigned for bad behavior. It required standing straight up, with arms folded across your chest. Not that bad, once you got used to it! I was placed with other kids on campus. Normally kids didn't react to kids placed on campus. Being the new kid on the block, I attracted stares. Curiosity, I guess.

The Jr. Counselor sat at Mr. O's. wooden desk. He was upset. Not so much for fighting. I accidently pushed him when he grabbed me. He didn't give me a chance to tell him that I was helping my brother. He shouted out to me a few times. Eventually, it registered. Kids quieted down. The Jr. Counselor shouted something in my direction again. I smiled.

He was up and in my face in a nanosecond. He made me raise my arms over my head. I did. The punch to my stomach doubled me over. I was attempting to catch my breath. He was bending down, yelling for me to stand up. I managed. I was hurting. Again, he yelled, "Put your arms up!" I didn't. I'm a fast learner. He settled for a few open palm-stinging slaps to my face. Dad never hit me in my face. I got the message. I managed to stand as straight as I could. He'd had enough with me. I had enough with him too. I stood, trying not to cry. Great place! Thanks, Dad!

Mr. O. came through the doors of the cottage. With his entrance, the noise levels reduced to a hum. Kids turned from me, returning to boxes, comic books, and board games quietly. Even the Jr. Counselor was quiet. Mr. O. directed everyone to their boxes before walking to where we were standing on campus. He released the other boys. They scampered to their boxes. Mr. O. spoke with the Jr. Counselor before telling him to leave.

Mr. O. stood directly in front of me. I almost peed in my pants. I was standing straight as I could. He stared down at me. I stared up at him. His blue eyes stared through me. I was anticipating the same treatment I'd received from the Jr. Counselor. After a hundred seconds, he spoke, softly, in a clear voice. You could hear a pin drop. Every eye in the cottage was on us. They were likely thankful, it was me, not them, on the receiving end of Mr. O.'s attention. I wished I was with them.

"John! Why were you fighting?" I explained as best I could. He listened. He told me fighting was not tolerated. Did I understand? You bet I did! He sent me to my box, good old number 29. My punishment restricted me to my box for the remainder of the day. The good news. I was relieved from campus time. Playtime resumed. I was glued to my box. Kids passed by, some speaking a few words and moving on. I didn't budge. Froggy sat down next to me. He didn't say anything. He didn't need to. He smiled. His face was a watershed of happiness. I smiled back.

Separated by age groups influenced separations. Like other newly arrived boys, we were entering our initial adjustments to the unknown. Family influences would slowly begin to dissolve, being replaced by influences dictated to the needs of The Mount. I quickly fell into line. Mr. O. was a fast read. He was stern, intimidating, a no-nonsense disciplinarian. He was my 'new dad.' I added him to the top of my list of people to avoid. 'Worked for me!'

Weekly Clothing Change

Clothing was interesting. We changed clothes weekly. Socks, pants, shirt, and underwear! Imagine wearing underwear a full week before changing. Skid marks were in fashion. Our underwear was a button down one piece, from the neck to mid-thigh. The back flaps of our underwear were held in place with buttons which had to be unbuttoned prior to taking a crap. Man, you had to be fast. Sweaters, hats, and coats rounded out clothes throughout the seasons. Soiled clothing was deposited in large laundry chutes weekly. The few exceptions were when a boy peed or crapped in their pants or when clothes were ripped. Kids wetting their beds changed as needed.

Our Sister assigned to Fifth cottage was tall, thin, quiet, and soft spoken. She carried a smile. She worked out of a small room in the rear of the cottage. She mended clothes. Her sewing machine could be heard when we were quiet. When Sister was around, Mr. O. was less intimidating!

Sister positioned laundry chutes weekly. We tossed soiled clothes into the chutes, exchanging them for fresh clothes. As for clean clothes, I can vouch for mixed colors. She did the best she could in assessing sizes as we received clothes. Nothing matched. We were 'poster boys.'

Tony the Shoemaker

He scared the living daylights out of me and, just about everyone else; at least on the small side. To say he wasn't intimidating would be lying. Tony, the shoemaker, mended and dispensed shoes. He worked in a standalone building. His personality matched the dark interior of the building.

Tony wasn't friendly – not even close. He yelled at every boy who faced him. He barely looked at anyone. He judged shoe sizes by our height – my opinion. He looked me over. From behind a counter, he reached into a box, filled with shoes. He picked out a pair, tossed them at me, shouting, "Keep moving." Tony, the shoemaker was a piece of work.

He couldn't compare with Grandpa. He was a shoemaker as well as a shoe repairman. I remember stopping off after school into his shoe shop. I picked out a seat in one of the high chairs where men sat, waiting for their shoes. I had a good view watching Grandpa behind the counter repairing shoes. His friends called him Mr. John. Few words were exchanged. They spoke mostly in Italian, often laughing at something one of them said. I was their audience.

Men arrived at the shoe shop. They asked Grandpa if their shoes were ready for pick up. With his back facing customers, without missing a beat and in broken English, and mostly in Italian, Grandpa shouted over his shoulder. "Do ya see 'em in da box?" If they replied no. Grandpa shouted, "They no ready. You come back."

Another bonus from visiting Grandpa's shoe shop was the smell of glue used to cement soles to the underside of shoes. The smell of glue permeated throughout the shoe shop. It wasn't long before I was feeling good. People often commented, "Johnny is such a happy boy." Loved that glue.

Fifth Cottage Candy Store

Another responsibility which fell to Sister Andrew was operating the candy store. The candy store was a small room, across from the sewing room. It was opened once a week for just a few hours. Kids were able to deposit money into an account which was monitored by Sister Andrew. From my box, I had a perfect view of the candy room. Sister Andrew standing behind the counter quietly exchanging candy for pennies, dimes, and nickels. I didn't have an account. Neither did Al or Bob.

Stories and Songs

Mr. O. read stories from Reader's Digest. I recall one. He spoke about a boy who had cancer. He read a part where the boy reached a stage when he was so weak, he couldn't cut through butter. That remained with me. Throughout the day, Mr. O. could be heard humming songs to himself. From time to time, he led a small group of 'his favorites' singing songs. Songs like 'To wake up in the morning, on mockingbird hill.' Oh boy!

Froggy Incident

We became good buddies, sometimes hanging together in and around the cottage. Froggy was the funniest kid I'd ever met; He wasn't a tough kid. He was a happy, smiling kid, always on the edge of a laugh. Foggy was well-liked by everyone. Well, almost everyone. An incident occurred once when we were gathered in our cottage. Froggy had several boys laughing loudly. The Jr. (junior counselor) wasn't amused. After shouts from the Jr. to quiet down, the laughing subsided before continuing. Froggy was placed on campus.

A few Jr. Counselors from other cottages entered our cottage. They spied Froggy standing on campus. They learned the reason why. They began teasing Froggy, causing him to laugh. Hell! Just the sight of Froggy with that big grin on his freckled face and all that orange hair was enough to crack anyone up. Mr. O. was on a day off. Sister Andrew was not around. What began as a funny situation soon turned ugly.

Jr counselors made him stand straight. He did. He was smiling; he always smiled. He was told to stop smiling. Froggy laughed. Kids laughed. Even some of the Jr counselors laughed. This didn't sit well with our assigned Jr. Counselor. He turned his attention to Froggy. He was made to hold his hands down and flat against the sides of legs. The Jr. Counselor slapped him across his face. Froggy still smiled. Each time he did, he received another slap across his face. Another Jr. Counselor deliberately caused Froggy to laugh. Froggy tried not to laugh; but, he did. Froggy received slaps across his face. The slaps became harder. Throughout the cottage, kids were becoming quiet.

Froggy broke down crying. Heavy tears rolled down his face. Sometimes, he smiled and cried at the same time. He couldn't help himself! A few kids were crying. The slaps continued. Froggy couldn't stop smiling. He stood straight up; his hands trembling at his side. Jr. Counselors took notice. Kids were not laughing. Many looked down at their feet or looked away. Muffled sniffles from Froggy continued. He was shaking and crying. His face was beet red. He wasn't laughing. He wasn't smiling. He'd been broken. Jr. Counselors attempted to calm him down. Slowly, he stopped crying. He was returned to his box. Froggy wasn't smiling! Jr. Counselors left the cottage.

Froggy entered The Mount as one of the youngest boys to be accepted; three or four years old. His days began in the youngest cottage which were supervised by Sisters. To my knowledge, Froggy never received visits. The Mount became his family. Visiting days were issues for Froggy. He never received visitors. Sometimes, he could be seen sitting with a kid's family visit. Throughout it all, Froggy had a smile for everybody.

Nights

My bed was located on the second dormitory floor of three levels. My bed was located next to an exit door which opened to the fire escape. It was different from the one in our apartment. It had a stairway versus ours which had a drop ladder. In case of an emergency, we were expected to climb down the fire escape stairs, most likely, yelling, shouting, and crying. All the stuff you'd expect from young kids. Just saying.

All three levels were exactly the same in width and length. The two top levels housed thirty beds to each side for a total of sixty white iron framed beds. Mr. O. led us through night-time prayers in the ground floor level. Once lined up at the foot of our beds, facing each other, Mr. O. wished us a good night. In return we wished a "Good night, Mr. O."

My first night, I pulled back the blanket and slid between the sheets. They felt cool. I pulled the blanket over me. The white iron famed beds were the same as the ones in the quarantine. Orange exit lights glowed over exit doors, fire escape, and the hallway.

Mr. O. usually left his door slightly open. The radio music was welcomed after lights out. Radio music from Mr. O's room reminded me of times when at home, Dad and Mom played radio music while we were in our beds. In time, hearing music from Mr. O's room was reassuring. The first night was an indoctrination. Kid's sobbing themselves to sleep. Others called out for Moms. Maybe they had a bad day; a punishment; missing family members or they were lonely. Some receded, hiding under their sheets. All were sending messages. Was anyone listening?

Jesus

Something unexpected happened to me as I laid in bed that first night in fifth cottage. Jesus name popped into my mind. His name was clear. I can't explain it other than that it had a calming effect on me.

I attended Parochial schools. Maybe my exposures to religious dos and don'ts had an effect on me. Sisters emphasized Jesus has a special love for children. At any rate, the incident remains with me to this day. When I found myself troubled with countless personal hardships, career decisions and disappointments; which were often, I'd reach out to Jesus for help. He never failed me. I can't explain it. It's between Him and me.

Bed Wetters

Waking up that first morning was interesting. The smell of urine was throughout the dorm. I checked myself. I was OK. Bed wetters were housed in the rear area of my dorm. Each morning, Mr. O's bellowing voice greeted us with "Good morning, boys." We jumped out of our beds. Lined up at the foot of our beds. Mr. O. asked bed wetters to step further out in front of their beds.

He didn't berate them. He instructed them to strip off their underwear and wet sheets from their beds. Sister Andrew appeared with a helper. They distributed clean underwear. Clean bed sheets and rubber sheets replaced the soiled ones. The rest of us changed weekly. I wonder would I have been better off wetting my bed, once in a while, just to receive a fresh change of underwear and sheets. Mr. O. asked bed wetters who didn't wet their beds to step out. He congratulated them. They'd be given one additional nighttime before being moved off the bed wetters list. Coming off the list entitled them to receiving normal work assignments.

Cleaning Crews

Shortly after arriving at sixth cottage, I was assigned to Sister Andrew's cleaning crew. Crews performed various jobs in cottages and assigned to outdoor areas as well. Most assignments were completed on a daily basis with Fridays and pre-holidays received extra attention. I didn't know what to expect. Cleaning toilets were included in Sister's cleaning crew, but, kids being punished and bed wetters were assigned by Mr. O. Consider; an average of 60 kids hitting the toilets before and after breakfast, lunch, and supper! Cleaning toilets was a nasty assignment. Kids cleaned them twenty-four-seven. My incident with hiding cigarettes certainly qualified me for toilet duty.

Sister Andrew assigned all other assignments, involving dusting, sweeping, dormitory duties, washing floors, changing bed linen, making beds and exchanging weekly changing of soiled clothes. Cleaning the main hall; sweeping floors, dusting windowsills, and wash up areas were considered easy assignments. Sister Andrew asked me. "Did you help cleaning at home?"

"I did, mostly on Saturdays."

"What did you clean, John?" I was doomed.

"The bathroom." I replied. Sister Andrew smiled. I was assigned to the Icky Poo crew. I had no idea what the Icky Poo crew was. I must have shown my concern. I replied with the only response I could come up with.

"What's Icky Poo?" As Sister Andrew walked me to the hall closet where cleaning supplies were stored, she explained my Icky Poo responsibilities.

We were interrupted. Three men approached Sister Andrew. I overheard them telling Sister they joined the army. I guess they were close to her at one time when they were assigned to fifth cottage. In later years, I realized they were referring to 'The Korean War' often referred to as a 'Police Action' involving the USA's participation. It was a horrible ground war, causing many American deaths and casualties.

My Icky Poo responsibilities included collecting used and nearly used soap bars from wash-up, shower stalls, and toilets areas. Sister Andrew shadowed me for a few rounds. Once on my own, I was unchallenged as I moved throughout the cottage on my collection route. I deposited used soap into a pail, I carried while making my rounds. Afterwards, I'd meet with Sister Andrew at a cleaning closet. After inspecting my collection of used soap. She and I repeated my rounds, replacing the slots with new bars of soap. The cycle was repeated daily.

Converting used soap bars into Icky Poo was cool. I filled a pail with used soap bars. I poured warm water over them. I mashed the soften soap bars together with my hands, adding warm water as needed. The mashed soap bars dissolved into a gooey liquid soap. Icky Pooh was born!

Icky Poo was The Mount's very own homemade liquid soap. It was used for washing floors, cleaning clothes, toilets, play areas, and dormitories. We were ahead of our time. I haven't a clue as to why I was selected by Sister Andrew to the Icky Poo crew but, all other assignments couldn't come close to being more interesting. Years later, while a recruit in the air force, I was assigned to the responsibility of 'Latrine Queen.' I monitored the cleaning of our barracks latrine, making certain we were always ready for inspection. Hey! It kept me out of KP duties. Thank you, Sister Andrew.

A Special Invitation?

Mr. O. rewarded kids with good school grades, ratting out kids, and other good deeds to spend a few minutes in his room before turning in. They were treated to cookies and milk. His invitations were known as 'goodies meetings.' I was invited to Mr. O's 'goodie' meeting. I haven't the faintest idea why I was invited. We watched TV. President-elect Truman was holding up a newspaper clipping. The famous photo announced 'Dewey elected President.' Oops! Being invited to Mr. O's room was twofold. For good behavior and good grades. Or, to receive punishment for bad behavior; inviting a spanking by Mr. O., sometimes referred to as Smoothie.

Dining Hall

The dining hall was located behind the quarantine building and church. Walkways leading from the cottages to the dining hall were covered with an overhang. Both sides of the walkway were open to the weather. As referred to, cottages were marked in order of age group, beginning with the oldest down to the youngest cottage. There weren't exceptions, regardless of the weather. Cold weather dictated a fast pace. A few hundred young boys marching in double lines. Spring, summer, and fall months were ideal. Though the heat and humidity of summers made me

Dining-Table Protocol

Eating in the dining hall was an eye opener. Five kids were assigned to a table. Food was delivered by kitchen crew walking open air racks down an aisle with tables on each side. Oval trays filled with meals were dispensed to each table by the kitchen crew. Tables were previously set with bread, milk or juice, and dessert.

The dining hall separated the big side kids from small side kids with partitioned expanding walls. Anything small side kids didn't eat was carried off to the big side kids. Once boys from both sides were positioned at assigned tables. A prayer was offered before each meal was served by a priest. Breakfast depending on the seasons; winter months, farina, or oatmeal were served.

Meals varied by days of the week. Example. Wednesday supper consisted of white rice with raisins and cinnamon. Slices of bread, pitcher of milk or juice, and a bowl of dessert completed the meal. Wednesday suppers of white rice, raisin, and cinnamon was my favorite meal. Sunday suppers were lighter than suppers served throughout the week. Cold cuts, bread, milk, cookies or ice cream were served.

New Boy Indoctrination

Receiving a fair share of food depended on who controlled the distribution of food. As the new boy at my table, I was expected to wait until everyone took their share of food. The kid in charge at my table didn't share food with others until he had his share which was more then what he should have received.

Counselors roaming between tables didn't enforce a fair share of distribution unless it was bought to their attention. At my table, I was not only last to receive food, but the supper pan reached me nearly empty. Being the new boy, my reaction was to not cause trouble; thinking that the next meals would be better once they got to know me.

It wasn't to be. Food passed to me regularly was an empty pan sitting in front of me. I hesitated trying to fit in. The kid in charge made sure others didn't pass me the main food tray until all of them received their shares. After a few meals I got the picture. Duh! Breakfast was easier. Cereal boxes were placed in bowls in front of each chair. Milk, poured from a pitcher, wasn't a problem. Lunch at times could be difficult. It was a warm up, of what I could expect at supper. Suppers soon became a serious problem for me. After a full day of classes and playtime activities, I arrived hungry for supper.

Synonyms

Food names were interesting. Bread were 'jots.' Potatoes were 'spuds.' Dessert was 'yum.' 'Sly fox' was swiping food from someone's plate before they could react. Everyone was fair game; new boys were taken advantage of. I caught on fast. At times, it got serious. I arrived for supper hungry and left supper hungry. I was hungry all the time. I didn't have treats stored in my bin. I didn't have money for candy

Sly Fox

Rule number one. When attempting to 'sly-fox' food, it's important to be faster than the person protecting his plate. I attempted to sly-fox a piece of chicken from the plate of the kid sitting next to me. He was faster. I was looking at a swinging fork stuck in my middle index finger on my right hand. The fork was stuck deep into my finger. The kid reached over. He yanked his fork from my finger. No one said a word. Now, not only was I hungry, I was in pain. I watched my finger trembling. Boys laughed – I was pissed. Lesson learned. To this day the middle index finger on my right hand is larger than the middle finger on my left hand.

Supper's continued to be difficult. Following my unsuccessful attempt at sly-foxing, the kids continued holding back food, until they had their fill. They became more comfortable in passing me nearly empty food pans. Now, more than ever, I was focused on protecting what food I had from sly-foxing. What food that did reach me was eaten as fast as possible. I was ignored. I almost lost a finger to sly fox, I was pissed. I didn't have friends to back me up.

My options were few. I could have alerted a counselor. That could cause the entire table to be placed on campus. 'Ratting out' wasn't an option. Besides, by doing so, would place me in a defensive position; I'd be known as a rat.

Counselors, brothers, and priests making the rounds, collecting uneaten food from our table without a glance. There was never left-over food to send to the big side tables. All food pans were passed to the kid controlling our table. He helped himself to as much food from the pan as he wanted before passing it around. I was getting more and more pissed. I attempted to get along. It was useless.

I looked for the kid in play areas. He always had friends with him. Simply put, I was assigned to his table. I was unlucky. An opportunity presented itself. Supper pans were being distributed. As the pan was being passed to the kid, I made a grab for the desert bowl. I grabbed the dessert bowl and placed it in front of me.

No one moved. The kid in charge told the boy next to me to take it away from me. I didn't release it. He told the kid again to take it. I held tightly to the dessert bowl. I stared at the kid. He didn't grab for the dessert bowl. I knew a counselor wouldn't be called. I asked for the pan of food. He wouldn't let the kid pass it to me. He was fuming! He told the kid again to pass the dessert bowl. I responded "Pass me the food pan first."
He told the kid, "Take the dessert bowl!"

OK! I spit into the dessert bowl as I passed it to the kid next to me. He didn't take it. He just stared at it. The table was quiet. The kid told me he was gonna get me in the play area. A fight! OK by me.

He was really pissed! I asked for the food pan again. He refused to let it be passed to me. We were at a standstill. I spit toward the bread plate. I think I missed. But it was enough to spook the other kids. One of them passed me the food pan. Geez, was that hard?

For the first time in days, I received a fair share of food. As for the dessert tray, the kid next to me dipped a spoon in the bowl, spooning around my contribution for a share of dessert. For the most part, it was left untouched. I reached for the bowl. No big deal. I had as much as I needed. It felt good to be full. The kid was a bully.

We exchanged stares in the play area for the next few days. It didn't go any further. We avoided each other. Eating supper was no longer a concern. I had food passed to me without interference. We didn't become friends. Our paths crossed in sports activities. We ignored each other. There was an unspoken understanding between us. It became a different situation after we transferred to the 'big side.' 'Reference Fink.'

Being stabbed with a fork, being punished for fighting positioned me to looking forward to Dad's visit to be taken out of 'The special school.' Weren't three weeks up? Al experienced a similar incident at his assigned table. A kid gave him a tough time. Another stood up for Al, shutting the kid down. Al was OK.

Bob became good at 'sly foxing.' In the beginning he was in the same position I was in. He made adjustments when it came to eating at his table. He recalls always being hungry. In fact, he and other boys would sneak to the rear of the dining hall where left over scraps were dumped in huge trash bins. Bob picked through the bins for scraps. I know, because I hit the bins too.

There were times when tables weren't set up by the time cottages were lined up outside the dining hall. When the staff set food items, milk, bread, etc. the doors were opened. It didn't happen often. But when it did, cottages were caught in cold winter days or hot summer days it was very uncomfortable. The worst was being caught in a freezing rain and blowing wind.

Summers

Summers invited vermin to appear in the dining halls. Fumigating the dining halls created an odor which was overwhelming. I could almost taste it as I entered the dining hall. Kids were overcome by the odor. Many couldn't eat or in my case, you just dealt with it.

Being younger, we didn't tolerate the fumigation odor as well as the older boys. They would feast at our expense. It was an over-load on leftover food from our tables delivered to the older boys. Roaches attempting to escape, crawled out of comfortable niches. They were on their backs, kicking their legs as they died. Occasionally, a mouse appeared running in crazy circles, struggling, and dying.

Bathrooms Showers and Wash up Areas

Bathroom, shower stalls, and wash areas were sectioned off by a common wall along one same side of the main floor of each cottage. Bathroom toilets and urinals, approximately twelve by fifteen feet, featured open urinals along one wall and toilet seats along two walls. Two small windows overhead provided ventilation. The bathrooms were in demand, especially following meals. Kids rushed to the bathroom. Lone lines formed with kids anxious to get to a toilet or urinal. 'Resembling the gold rush of the early eighteen hundreds. Being prepared when nature called required teamwork. Kids with urgent needs were mostly permitted to cut ahead of others waiting to use a toilet seat or urinal. Kids self-monitored the process.

A daily occurrence was kids from play areas running and yelling "Look out, I gotta go." It was funny, watching a kid fiddling with unbuttoning back-flaps of his underwear as he raced toward the toilets with his pants and hanging back flaps being held up as he raised for the bathroom.

Returning from dining and play areas was somewhat organized and funny while being challenging to those in need. Kids formed lines behind each other, moving forward as each toilet or urinal became vacant. Kids crapped, farted, and peed nonstop. Nice visual!

Winter months were particularly difficult. Kids played outdoors in spite of inclement weather. Gloves! Yeah, sure. We endured chapped hands, knuckles, and cracked lips. Vaseline was our best friend. Mr. O. made certain Vaseline was available as needed, especially after showers and wash ups. Vaseline was king.

Showers

Al, Bob, and I always bathed in a bathtub. In The Mount, Saturday weekly showers replaced the bathtub. Changing underwear was scheduled for Saturdays as well. After wearing and playing in the same clothes for a week, showers were welcomed. Underwear took a beating. Brown-skid mark underwear were common reminders of struggles when unbuckling rear flaps.

Saturday night showers were welcomed. The shower room had overhead piping with thirty shower heads. Mr. O. controlled the water temperature as evenly as possible. He ran water through the pipes until they reached a proper temperature, especially in cold winter months.

Not so with Jr. counselors. Boys were positioned directly under the shower heads. Moans from the boys standing under cold water showerheads echoed throughout the cottage. The moans stopped when warm water poured through the showerheads. The first grouping of boys were guinea pigs.

Mr. O. rewarded groups who progressed in an orderly and quiet manner as they prepared for wash up or showers. It was a way to get everyone within groups to cooperate. Rewards were based on entering and leaving wash up or showers in a quiet manner. Rewards were quietly reading comic books, playing checkers and rearranging personal items stored in box bins as quietly as possible.

Night Time Wash Ups

Evening wash-up was similar to lining up for showers. Thirty kids lined up to each side of washbasins, resembling troughs. My first toothbrush was hanging on a hook next to my number 29. I removed my tooth brush and towel from the hook. We faced each other across the troughs washbasins. A large can of dried powder was passed around. I watched the kid next to me pour tooth powder from the can into his palm. He mixed water into the tooth powder. I did the same. I brushed my teeth. The tooth powder was tasteless.

Dad's First Visit

Dad finally showed up sometime in November. It had been several weeks into our stay at The Mount. What was in my mind should have been a good memory, wasn't. I was sitting on my box, playing checkers with the boy next to me. I heard a whistle. I knew that whistle. It couldn't belong to anyone but Dad. It was the same one he used when calling us from our playroom or from anywhere.

I looked up, turned my head toward where the whistle came from. Dad was standing next to Mr. O. He was looking right at me. I recall that look today as I saw it then. Dad was looking straight at me, smiling. I had an unexplainable feeling! Mr. O. Uncle Frank, and Dad stood together at the entrance to my cottage. Dad was wearing his black winter overcoat, his hat leaning to the side of his head. Both of his hands were tucked into his overcoat pockets. I flew off my box, running, literally flying. I jumped into his arms. I was crying. I was happy. I was going home! Three weeks of 'special school' were over.

Dad seemed to be caught off guard. I was hugging him, both arms tightly wrapped around him. He was speaking to me. It's a blur. I loved his voice. I can't recall his exact words. I looked up at Mr. O, Uncle Frank, and Dad. I managed to say, between tears which were beginning to flow from my eyes. "I'm going home."

"Not yet, Johnny." It was Dad's voice. I looked up at him. He was speaking to me. "Not yet, Johnny" began registering with me. I stared up at Dad.

I muttered, "Isn't it three weeks, Dad? Isn't it three weeks yet?" Dad was awkward. I don't recall him answering me. He and Mr. O were speaking to each other. I remained clinging to Dad. I shot glances at Uncle Frank and back to Dad. "Not yet, Johnny" didn't register yet.

Just like that. All of maybe two or three minutes. Dad released himself from my death grip. He was gone. Just like that – no goodbye. Did he visit Al and Bob? They can't remember. I stared at the door. I can't remember him leaving. Dad was gone. I was a mess.

I looked up at Mr. O. *What just happened!* His dark eyes stared down for just a moment before his damn voice of authority hit me like a brick. "John, go back to your box." I cried and sobbed through wash up, evening prayers, eventually sobbing myself to sleep. Dad's only words to me that night were "Not yet, Johnny."

I wasn't going home. Al and Bob weren't going home. Dad's visit with Uncle Frank was the beginning of visits to us. He was always accompanied by a relative or a friend. From then on, questions regarding going home or about our mom were consistently met with non-responses from Dad. He settled into a pattern ignoring our questions. We were young, naïve, and confused. In time, he wore us down.

Dad was already committed to us and Mom remaining where he placed us. A new Aunt was introduced as Aunt Dolly. Dad was bent on replacing our Mom with Aunt Dolly. He indoctrinated us throughout ensuing years by exposing Aunt Dolly to us on his visits. Simply put, it was self-serving on his part. It almost worked.

Dad continued ignoring questions on when we'd be leaving The Mount. He never brought Mom into our visits with him. Our families supported Dad in not ever bringing up Mom with us. Eventually we were positioned into adjusting to The Mount's regulations. Leaving the Mount in three weeks was a non-issue. Unbeknownst to us, we faced eight plus years. Mom faced eleven years. Mom and us were in for a long run. Were we doomed?

Mom forcefully removed by The Men in White in our presence provided Dad options. He might have told us. "Mom was sick." "She needed to get well." "Mom loves you." "She will be better soon." Could that have been so hard? An explanation along those lines might have made sense to us. We were young and trusting. Assistance from uncles and aunts, emphasizing to keeping us together as a family was an option. Dad didn't take that route. We adjusted to cottage's rules, regulations, counselors, dining hall, friendships, grammar school, trade schools, sports, and growing into a world devoid of family influences.

Dad's visits settled into bi-monthly visits on Saturdays. We gathered together at the quarantine building, where it all began. He arrived with a friend, or a borrowed car. We'd keep our eyes focused on cars approaching the quarantine building. In the early years gathering together wasn't a problem. All of us were assigned to the small side.

Transferring to the big side posed a challenge to gather us together at one time. The big side offered less supervision. We were left to ourselves. Dad demanded we still meet at the quarantine building. Eventually, while out and about on the campus grounds, one of us would be missing. Dad had a fit. He'd drive all over the campus searching for one of us. Maybe if we lived together under one roof as a family, we wouldn't be out and about. Geez.

In the early years, while on the small side, we wouldn't have trouble being together for Dad's visits. It did bother me knowing when he wasn't visiting us. Other kids received visits. I avoided being in areas where kids and their visitors gathered. I'd busy myself hanging out in the gymnasium.

Newly arrived kids lined the road leading from Hyland Boulevard onto The Mount's grounds. New kids lucky enough to receive family visits often were overcome with tears, especially when they realized they'd remain in The Mount as their families left the grounds. Still others didn't received visits. They cried. Some remained on the side of the road long after visits were over. Eventually, they were directed to their cottages.

In time kids make adjustments, just as we did. I came to expect non-visits from Dad. Dad's visits were the highlight of my week. If he showed up late, I'd be a mess. We looked for a car with Dad in it. All was good. As the car came to a stop, Dad smiled, waving his hand to us. The excitement cannot be explained. My eyes welled up with tears. Dad had that effect on me.

Many times, after Dad dropped us off by the quarantine building, I'd run to my cottage, kneel on my box, and watch through the windowpane looking for Dad's car disappearing down the road, away from us. I watched as long as possible. The empty feeling cannot be described. I busied myself on the playground or in cottage games. Eventually, my sadness was put aside. It was always rough to be alone.

In the early days, we'd ask about Mom. Dad's mood changed. He'd change the subject. He didn't answer us. We were kept in the dark. We were confused. Dad didn't realize we couldn't forget Mom that easily. Or for that matter, ever. Dad, by ignoring us, set himself up for the day when he would have to come to terms with our questions.

In Between Dad's Visits

Between Dad's visits, I made adjustments. I hung around with kids, lining up for visits and handouts along the road leading up into The Mount. Arriving cars slowing down; passing candy out open car windows to kids. I ran alongside cars with my hands outstretched hoping to receive candy. People in the cars knew kids with their hands out weren't receiving visits. Kids wearing a sad face also worked. Cars slowed down. Hands reached out from the cars, offered candy, before driving on to visit their kids.

A few times I was invited by a kid to join him on their visit. It felt good to be with them. There were few questions asked. The families were nice. They shared whatever they had. They knew the drill. On the other hand, Dad didn't encourage us to invite kids on our visits. So, we didn't. Anyway, it meant a bag of Hershey's candy kisses were shared between us. To boot, they were individually wrapped, making it easy to barter with.

Holiday Home Visits

Holidays, especially at Christmas time, were special. The Mount was cleared out throughout the week of Christmas. Kids looked forward to home visits for a few days. Our first home visit occurred in the second or third year after entering The Mount. Dad picked us up at the quarantine building.

He took us to Grandpa and Grandma's apartment. Walking into their apartment was surreal. Just a few years ago, we each received small paper bags with candy from Grandpa and Grandma as we left their apartment for school. Ultimately to 'The Red-Brick building.' Ahh!

Aunts, uncles, and cousins greeted us with hellos, hugs, kisses, and handshakes as we entered the apartment. Grandpa greeted us with giant hugs, rubbing his moustache against our cheeks. Grandma followed with kisses and hugs. Relatives were limited to "How are you?" "Gee, you're getting tall" "Eat something." Everyone was happy. It felt awkward. How did they really feel? Seeing Dad bringing his three boys from an orphanage to visit with them on Christmas Day. How about Mom? Where was she on Christmas Day? How screwed is that?

The small kitchen was packed tight with aunts, uncles, cousins, and Grandpa and Grandma. We were treated to loud voices, laughter, and greetings as Dad led us through the kitchen toward the rear of the apartment where their small living room overlooked Sixth Street.

We passed Grandpa and Grandma's bedroom. My eyes went to the top of Grandma's dresser. Lit candles in small red and white glass holders surrounded statues of Mary, Jesus, and Saint Joseph. The candles were the only light in the windowless bedroom. It was eerie.

Dad walked us to the rear living room. The heat rising from a portable gas heater as we entered the small living room felt good. A small Christmas tree, Grandpa's small B&W TV and a few chairs completed the room. Dad turned on the black and white T.V. before returning to the kitchen. We had the room to ourselves.

Envelopes were tucked in between branches of the Christmas tree. A closer look revealed Christmas green and red colored gift envelopes. Dad returned with uncles and aunts. We were encouraged to search for envelopes with our names written on them. Uncles and aunts gathered around as we opened our gift envelopes. They smiled as we removed crisp new dollar bills from our gift envelopes. Aunts kissed us. Uncles shook our hands. Dad collected our dollar bills, saying to no one in particular. "I'll hold them for the boys."

Everyone returned to the kitchen where drinks, pastries, and family catch-ups resumed. We remained in the rear living room with empty Christmas gift envelopes. I could have used the money to open a candy account in the commissary store in fifth cottage.

A cousin wandered into the room. As he passed me, I jokingly jabbed him in his stomach; just kidding around. He returned to the kitchen. He returned with his father, our uncle. "What's going on in here? Who's hitting who?" Looking directly at me.

"I was just kidding around."

"You better behave yourself. You don't want me to tell your father, do you?"

I mumbled "No." A last look from our uncle wasn't anywhere close to one of Dad's 'laser looks.'

The incident bothered me. Slowly, little by little, I was growing apart from our family.

Grandma prepared meals on a wood burning stove. Newspaper was inserted into a small area. Wood scraps were placed on paper and lit. Small blue charcoal chips were added to the fire. There you have it. No gas, no electricity, just a wood burning stove, producing delicious tasting meals.

Grandma controlled her kitchen. As a matter of fact, all our aunts controlled their kitchens. Our Uncle Bob was the exception. I recall watching him rolling dough into shapes of Italian holiday cookies. Uncle Bob and our future Aunt Toni were engaged. They were super nice to us.

Grandma prepared her traditional Italian meal. Homegrown canned red tomatoes from the garden were added to a large pot. Basil, parsley, garlic, onion, and other herbs were mixed into the tomato gravy. Italian sausages, hot and sweet, a piece of pork and meatballs, were added into the gravy. Everything simmered for hours before homemade pasta, boiled *al dente*, completed the meal.

Uncles crowded around Grandma at her stove waiting to dip ends of hard Italian bread into the simmering thick red tomato gravy. Hot gravy dipped through their fingers as they thrust gravy-soaked Italian bread into their mouths. Eventually, Grandma chased them away from her stove.

At dinner adults gathered around the table. It was a tight squeeze. Cousins ate at a bridge table placed off to the side. Full plates of pasta and meats were served to adults first. Aunts filled our plates. Grandpa's homemade wine, prepared from grapes was stored in bottles in the basement. A few bottles left unsealed for the wine to oxidize, into a red Italian wine used in salads. Uncles and aunts laughed, ate, drank wine, and occasionally called out to us. "Who wants more pasta, meatballs, or sausages?" It was a special time.

The smell of ripe home-grown red tomatoes simmering into a deep tomato gravy, flavored with meatballs, hot and sweet sausages has the same effect on me today as it did then. Following our traditional Italian Christmas dinner, Uncles relaxed. Aunts washed, dried, and reset the table for Italian pastries, fruit, and assorted nuts. Espresso, anisette, and wine joined the second onslaught. We ate pastries and returned to the living room where we watched TV; occasionally looking into branches for missed Christmas gift envelopes. Nothing!

All too soon, Dad gathered us for goodbyes to Uncles, Aunts, Grandpa, and Grandma. Just like the morning when we left their apartment for school, Grandma made sure we had Christmas candy and homemade cookies to take with us. This time, we knew where we were heading to. Our Christmas visit with our family began in the morning and ended in late afternoon on the same day we arrived.

Spending Christmas with families was popular and looked forward to by kids. We weren't alone, with one difference. Our visits were one-day visits. The majority of kids remained with families throughout Christmas week before being returned to The Mount. Some kids were lucky to be selected by families willing to share their family holidays with them.

Kid's left behind received toys and holiday treats from The Mount. A special Christmas supper was served for both sides. Ice cream was a must. The Mount did the best they could for boys and girls left behind throughout the holidays. Sisters sang carols, many in Latin, at Christmas services.

At any rate, Dad drove us to the Staten Island Ferry. He gave us money for the bus ride to The Mount. It may have come out of our Christmas envelopes. Just saying. Kids who remained behind met us as we arrived back at The Mount. We shared treats with them. I hid candy and cookies under clothes and stuff in my bin.

Christmas
New York Telephone Ladies

The New York Telephone Ladies arrived each year, a week before Christmas. They always arrived with Christmas gifts for every kid on the small side. I remember receiving a Flashlight. Boys from the sixth cottage received a pen & pencil set. The flashlights were a hit. As soon as it became dark, flashlights crisscrossed the night sky; quite a sight. Eventually, batteries wore out. Dark nights returned.

Kids from the small side didn't have money for batteries. Older boys who had money from various jobs could afford batteries. Bartering for flashlights began immediately. Flashlights were sold and bartered for. Older boys had the advantage. Most likely offering pennies in exchange for a flashlight.

A Close Call

A special Christmas-themed show performed in the basement of the Church by the Telephone Ladies was looked forward to each year. Everyone was invited. Christmas carols and Christmas skits were performed. Santa Claus closed the performance, arriving in his sled pulled by Santa's helpers (Telephone Ladies) attired in reindeer costumes. Santa waved shouting Ho-Ho-Hos to one and all.

I joined a small group of kids. We slipped away from our cottage as we approached the Church. We hid in a nearby shrubbery by a basement window. We were told, the Telephone Ladies changed in the basement. We were going to spy on them as they changed into costumes. A bad idea. "Really!"

I heard voices. Counselors walking close to where we were hiding. It was too late to slip away. We hugged close to the ground. A few kids panicked. They made a run for it. The counselors chased after them, yelling for them to stop. I wiggled further into the shrubbery, hugging the ground as close as I could. I heard kid's being rounded up. I stayed put.

It became quiet. I crept out from hiding. I circled the church, to the opposite side, where boys from the big side were arriving. I entered the church with them. No one stopped me. I slid into an aisle where my fifth cottage group was. I hardly recall the show. I was expecting a tap on my shoulder by a counselor. The show ended. I walked back to our cottage with my group. Kids caught were placed on campus. They didn't turn me in to the counselors. No one gave me up. I was lucky.

The New York Telephone Ladies Christmas gifts and Christmas performance will remain a highlight of Christmas in The Mount. We looked forward to their arrival. For many it was their only Christmas.

Basketball

I played with the small side basketball teams. My speed made up for not being tall. I was assigned to the house league basketball team. I played for Coach Doc. He was a big man. He was soft spoken. He was a stickler for practice drills, repeating over and over until we had the drills down pat.

He didn't bother with complicated plays. Coach Doc emphasized fast breaks. He drilled positions into us, over and over until we were automatically assuming our positions. I played forward positions with another kid, Ray. When a rebound was passed to one of us; we were off to the races, trading passes as we raced for our basket, ending up near the basket for one of us to take the shot. That was fun.

Our team had another player, also named Ray. He was the best shooter on our team. He scored baskets anywhere within the foul line circle. He made the difference in many of our wins. We had another advantage. Doc emphasized shooting from the foul line, underhand. All in all, we were a well-balanced basketball team. As for playing basketball on the big side, I played with kids bigger than I was. My advantage was knowing kids who played with me on the small side. Hanging out with them in the gymnasium, playing on pick up teams made my adjustments easier than most.

Cottage Games

Countless games of checkers, chess, and ping-pong along with games of chance occupied playtime. A popular game required rolling a marble though a small opening hole in an upside-down top of a candy box. Rolling a marble though the opening could increase an inventory of toys, comics, baseball cards, candy, and pennies. Missing the opening cost whatever was put up by a kid rolling the marble. It was fun watching a ringer, someone whose aim was good, roll for a win.

I played when an item was something I wanted, I was willing to take a chance on losing whatever I put up against the item I was rolling for. Outdoor games: baseball, softball, racing, and stickball were played on an asphalt covered playground. Father Kenny could be found hitting baseballs to kids scattered in the outfield or shooting hoops with them.

Downhill 'In Line' Roller Skating

My favorite outside sport was downhill inline roller skating. Valuable possessions were roller blades, a single roller skate and a skate key. I didn't have either. I traded for a skate key. A skate key was needed to tighten clamps onto sneakers. Some kids had skates but, not a skate key. I earned pennies from kids by lending them my skate key. I used the pennies to buy a single skate. Now, I rented a skate key and a single skate. I had enough pennies to buy/trade for another skate. No more balancing on one skate. I joined the inline downhill skaters.

The asphalt was perfect for roller-skating. The skating area from the top to the bottom was naturally slanted toward ending the front of our cottages. It was perfect for downhill roller-skating. Throughout spring, summers, and fall seasons, kids lined up for inline downhill racing. Skaters formulated into teams on the top of the hill. I gained confidence in my speed; enough to be noticed and picked to ride with the fastest groups. Teams were made up of six to eight riders to skate as a team.

Trust was important for team members. Leaning into turns in unison required feeling the ride and speed as one unit as they raced downhill. In order to gain as much speed as possible, team members crouched as low behind each other, holding on to the waist of the person in front of you. Once under way, the objective was to generate as much speed as possible. We'd zip through tight turns, wider loops, and, sometimes, complete circles, gaining as much speed as possible roaring toward the bottom of the run.

Gaining speed, turning, looping, and weaving in and out of kids was exciting, hearing "Here they come." Hearing the roar of roller wheels grinding against asphalt was thrilling. The roar of skaters in line had a positive effect on kids playing in the area; encouraging them to jump out of the way.

Not being able to see over the person in front of you added to the excitement. Passing over the asphalt pavement, hitting bumps and open cracks required rapid adjustments by lead skaters. They were fearless. They were known to 'let it rip' as we raced down the slanted pavement as fast as possible.

Counselors monitoring the play areas were alert to downhill skaters. Occasionally, they attempted to slow down the speed of roller-skating lines. One time our team leader became so excited, he failed to signal us to slow down. We were a 'run-away skating team' roaring toward the bottom of the run. I sensed we were moving really fast; too fast as we approached the bottom of the run. I looked up instinctively.

Several riders were shouting and rising up from crouches alerting team skaters. We hung onto each other, fighting to slow down as we neared the bottom of the run. Our team leader attempted to turn horizontally before hitting the bottom of the slope. Too late.

We must have looked strange as we leaned together trying not to cross the open channel that carried rainwater away from the cottages. We slid into the channel sideways, scattering like falling feathers in all directions. Counselors ripped into us. We were laughing. We weren't bruised. We were rounded up. Our team leader had his skates taken from him for a period of time Cool run! Roller Coasters, move over!

Busted

Selling cigarettes at The Mount was risky. Older boys went around the back of the gymnasium to smoke. I ventured toward the rear of the gymnasium. A look-out chased me away. Over a period of time and running into the same look-outs, I was offered to be a holder. My reward was candy. As a holder I held a few butts in my pockets. Before the bell rang, I'd return the butts to the look-outs.

One day, playing with other kids on the playground, I lost track of time. The bell sounded. I didn't have time to return the butts. I watched the older boys returning to their cottage. They saw me. They ignored me. I had their butts in my pants' pocket. I could have ditched them. I didn't. I returned to my cottage box. I hid the butts under whatever toys, comic books, and bits of clothing I had in my seat box. Does tobacco smell? Duh! It didn't take long for Mr. O. to begin making the rounds, stopping by each boy's seat box, sniffing and continuing. He stopped by my seat box. He had each boy to the side of me

142

open their seat boxes. Nothing! Mr. O. continued down the line. That was close!

As I exited from our nightly wash up area, Mr. O. pulled me aside. "John. Walk to your seat box." I was doomed. My stomach said as much. "Open your seat box." I did as I was told. Mr. O. laid a hand on my shoulder. "Stand back, John." I nearly tossed my cookies. Sanding and shaking as Mr. O. stared down at me with his laser-like blue eyes. "John. Do you have anything to say?"

I looked up at Mr. O. "No," I replied.

Mr. O. met my response with a thin smile. "Empty your box." I did, slowly, maybe wishing the cigarette butts would disappear. I was shaking. I emptied my contents onto the box next to mine. The cigarette butts fell out from the pile. "John. Where did you get these cigarettes?"

"I found them." I couldn't believe the words were coming from my mouth.

"John. Where did you find them?"

"Behind the gymnasium." I responded.

"Who was with you, John?"

"No one."

"Why were you behind the gymnasium?"

"I don't know," I responded in a weakened voice.

"What were you going to do with the cigarettes, John?"

Again, I responded, "I don't know."

"Tell me the names of boys who were smoking behind the gymnasium, John."

I responded, "I don't know anybody who smokes." Oops!

Mr. O. picked up the cigarettes. I was screwed. I had the attention of the cottage. It was quiet. Froggy shot me a sad smile from across the hall. Following night prayers, I was separated and made to stand just outside Mr. O's room. Often Mr. O played music from his room, leaving the door open, permitting soothing music to reach our ears as we lay in bed. Along with music, he permitted a few kids to sit in his room, watching black and white T.V. on a small screen.

This time was no different. Except, I wasn't invited to the party. I thought maybe my punishment was just that. To be made standing outside his open door while kids enjoyed T.V. and treats hosted by Mr. O. Being punished meant I'd receive campus time. I could handle standing up straight, with arms folded or held down along the side of my legs. No big deal. Boys filed out of Mr. O's room. A few smiled as they passed me.

143

Encouraging? The voice from the 'inner sanctum' called out.

"Come in, John. I need to know the names of boys who smoke or who were with you behind the gymnasium."

I responded. "I found the butts." Not ratting out the boys assured me of avoiding a possible beating from them. More importantly, not being known as someone who ratted out.

Mr. O. sat on the edge of his bed. He made me pull my underwear down, The ones with button down flaps in the rear. This required unbuttoning the top of my one-piece underwear flap. He mumbled something, "John, lay across my lap." I felt his hand on my butt. He patted my butt a few times. Nice touch! Rapid spanking followed. His hand was a human Gatling-gun. I was now officially a member of Mr. O's 'smoothie club.'

Several weeks later, after transferring to the sixth cottage, I joined the boys smoking at the rear of the gymnasium. A few of them were smoking from Corn Cobb pipes, a new fad? The pipes were purchased from a small candy store run by an old couple in a small town near The Mount. Boys from The Mount had to sign their names to a ledger when the purchased Corn Cobb pipes. They signed their names, "Superman, Mighty Mouse," and others including a slew of misspelled names. There was never a follow-up.

Intramural Sports

Bob setting the football – John kicking
'Lightweights' – Obviously, not cut out for football

Playing in house leagues prepared many kids to join varsity team sports, playing in off-campus away games against teams with similar backgrounds throughout the area. Football was a popular sport. The Mount's Varsity Football team was strong, tough with win-win attitudes. The games drew large crowds at home, as well as in away games.

Intramural sports on the big side were open to all boys, regardless of skill levels. That being said, the competition was advanced. I was still small for my age and underweight. I was able to get by competing on the small side. I met my match on the big side. In spite of not excelling in sports on the big side, I was able to enjoy basketball, stickball, and softball, making my transition to the big side easier.

Al

Al played defense as a linebacker on the varsity football team. He recalls playing against one of the toughest running backs on the opposing team. Al took his position on defense. He had an up-close experience. The ball was snapped, the running back broke through the offensive line, charging toward Al at full speed. Al held his ground. Duh! They collided. The player was upended over Al. Al got credit for the tackle. Al still feels good about that hit.

Al played baseball – third base position. In one game, he slammed three home runs. His shining moment! In the same game, a hard hit toward third base was intercepted by Al's outstretched hand, the one without a glove. The ball hit his finger straight on, breaking it in three places. Ouch!

A multiple broken finger! Al was taken to the hospital. He remained for three days. Before he was discharged, he was given an invoice. Al was not amused. He was earning $2.50 cents a month, working at the infirmary. He simply walked out.

Bob

He's the shortest of the three of us. What he lacked in height, he made up in determination. He played intramural sports. A little basketball. No pun intended. He played football. He was the quarterback – seriously? Considering his height and weight, that had to be interesting. As pointed out, he was determined. Baseball was his game. He was comfortable playing infield positions. He was a good hitter. He ran the bases fast. To this day, he plays an infield position in a senior baseball league.

John

I played intramural sports. Basketball, stickball, and football. I almost made the baseball team as a second baseman. I was comfortable fielding balls hit my way and had a strong arm. But, I messed up. I was at the gymnasium with teammates for the coach. I sneaked off to the side of the gymnasium for a smoke. Smoking cigarettes was a no-no. I grabbed a drag or two from a kid's butt. Unfortunately, coach turned the corner on his way to our team. He spotted me smoking. I was dismissed from the team – on the spot. Geez.

Christmas Nativity Manger

Each year a wooden nativity manger was placed just off Hyland Boulevard. It had statues of the Virgin Mary, Saint Joseph, the tree Kings with camels and sheep positioned in and around Baby Jesus. Motorists occasionally stopped to enjoy the manger and on occasion they placed a few coins into a wooden box placed near the manger by enterprising boys from the big side. When it was removed, it was replaced with another donation box. It was back and forth between big side boys removing donated coins from the wooden box and counselors removing the wood box.

Baseball with Dad... Again!

Old habits are hard to forget. Dad's visits evolved into arriving, gathering us into the car, a short car ride to a dead-end street where Dad parked the car. We jumped out. Dad popped the trunk. We grabbed gloves, bat, and a baseball. Sound familiar? Only this time, Dad wouldn't let us take turns hitting the baseball. The streets were narrow and lined with parked cars. Besides, we never knew where a ball hit by us would end up.

Dad hit the baseball to us. He called out for us to "get after the ball." After hitting to us, he yelled, "Don't let it go into the sewer." or "Hells Bells," when a baseball rolled past us, toward a sewer opening. He'd revert to his old self, "Get after it, boys. Oh no – oh no – oh no." "Don't let it roll into the #X@# sewer." That's the Dad we knew.

Dad was determined and prepared to retrieve the baseball from the sewer. He removed a stick with a small net attached to it from the truck of the car. Dad laid flat on his stomach and lowered the stick as far as he could through the sewer. He swung that stick back and forth. Sometimes he was able to snag the baseball. Most times, he wasn't. It was funny to hear him mumbling, as he fished for the baseball.

Following 'infield practice,' we'd head back to The Mount. We were handed a bag of chocolate kisses to share. Receiving candy signaled the end of Dad's visit with us. We went our separate ways, until the next visit. A visit usually lasted no more than an hour's time. Hey! Dad had things to do.

Our time, our dependence became attached to the needs of The Mount. We migrated to cottage activities, playground, and sports I played with the basketball team. It was exciting. We practiced throughout the week. Games were played on Saturdays. I asked Dad if he would come to see me play basketball on a Saturday morning. He said he'd come.

Saturday arrived. I was in the gymnasium, dressed in my basketball uniform. Al and Bob waited for Dad in front of the quarantine building. I peeked out the gym doors searching for Dad's car. I watched as cars turned in from Hyland Boulevard, hoping Dad would be in one of them. He said he'd see me play.

Finally, I walked to the quarantine building where Al and Bob were waiting. The basketball game was played. They won the game; without me. I missed my basketball game. I was a mess. As I watched the visiting team leaving the gymnasium area, Dad, with Uncle Frank, arrived.

I was upset. Dad looked at me. "Johnny, is that your basketball uniform?"
"Dad, you missed my basketball game." I remained in my basketball uniform throughout the visit. I was in a sour mood. Dad knew it.

Eventually, we were dropped us off at the quarantine building. Dad remained in the car. Missing my basketball game meant so much to me. Having my dad miss me playing in the game, meant even more to me. I wanted him to see me play. We were both upset. Uncle Frank got out of the car. As he passed the bag of chocolate kisses to Al, he said to me. "John, don't be upset with your dad. Do you know? He has trouble sleeping at night, thinking about you boys."
I responded, "He missed my basketball game."

Three Weeks

No Longer an Issue

"Three weeks." "A special school." Really! Actually, we realized we were living in an orphanage; pure and simple. Typically, Dad didn't feel it necessary to soften the blow. Would it have alleviated my confusion? Probably not. Did he think we'd be OK living in an orphanage? Was Mom OK living in a mental facility? Just saying. After a while, I stopped saying we were going home in three weeks; especially when it dawned on me, other kids in The Mount experienced similar situations and were still in The Mount. Duh.

And, there was Froggy's time spent in The Mount. He never complained about leaving or not receiving visits. He made adjustments. We were in the same boat. Neither of us were going anywhere. "Three weeks in a special school was a lie. Another thought. Living with Uncles and Aunts; Growing up in the same neighborhood with cousins? Dad passed on their offers.

He opted for an orphanage where we were placed in separate cottages, exposed to rules, regulations, enforced and supervised by counselors. What the hell was he thinking? Ultimately, Dad's decision eliminated our families from both sides. 'The Mount versus a Family.' Parental guidance all but disappeared. Dad's stubbornness, lies, withholding Mom's condition, and years of forced adjustments resulted in anger, guilt, isolation, and continuing confusion in the four of us. Dad once said. "The boys had it rough." Really?

Visits

Siblings and family visits were exchanged on Sundays. Thursdays provided visits from boys to the girls side of The Mount. Family visits reinforced relationships. We didn't have a sister. Would Dad have placed his daughter in The Mount? Anyway. If I had been told there were girls in the special school; Hell! Three weeks! No problem, Dad.

New Kid

Sunday. Siblings mixed in with families visiting kids as they gathered throughout the cottage areas. I was hanging out in my cottage. I noticed a kid crying. He was sitting with a girl on his box. I approached them. I don't know why. I just did. The girl was older, a teenager? She was speaking to him. She was hugging him.

I approached them. She looked up and smiled. She said she was visiting her brother. I sat with them. She asked how long had I been in the home. Home. No, no, this was an orphanage. Did I like being here? I didn't correct her. I told her; it was OK. That I had older and younger brothers; who lived in cottages next to the one we were sitting in. I didn't say much.

I remained sitting with them. No particular reason why. Her brother was a new kid in The Mount. He hugged her. He was a mess. He didn't speak to me. She continued holding him, speaking softly to him. Her eyes were moist.

Whistles announced the end of visiting hours. He begged her. "Please don't go." She kept telling him she'd be back. He hugged her more tightly. She wiped tears from his eyes. Kids were returning to the cottage. She asked me to be friends with him. I nodded.

She got up to leave. He got up with her, hugging her close to him. He begged her not to leave him. She hugged him. She kissed him. She gently broke away from him. He seemed to give up, crying softly as he released his arms from her. I watched her leave our cottage. She never looked back!

He sat down, hunched over, crying. I didn't know what to say! I can't explain the feeling. I felt bad for him. I didn't want her to leave him. I didn't know her name. I never saw her again. I never saw him again. I returned to my box.

Just like so many of us, he disappeared into the system. Maybe he got lucky and was discharged from The Mount. The brief time spent with them affected me. I had a flash back to Dad's first visit! I was confused. Occasionally, I witnessed kids released to their family. It was a happy time for the kids. There were hugs, tears, and smiles. It was difficult to see kids leaving the Mount.

Adjustments

Priests, Sisters, Brothers, and Administrative Staff formulated an effective communication between them and us. They became our family. Releasing us only when we were released from them. Depending on the amount of years spent in The Mount determines a boy or girl's success in what has been learned, observed and retained once released to the outside world.

Days became weeks. Weeks became months. Months became years. My adjustments hardened, matching policies, regulations, disappointments and performance. My behavior channeled to conforming with the least amount of effort, to conforming. Does that make sense?

Between Dad's visits, I positioned myself to visit with other boys' families. One boy stood out. He agreed to take me on his family visits if I agreed to return any candy given to me by his family after they left. Needless to say, I agreed and, ate as a much as I could before the family left. Funny!

Within a few years, Al was transferred to the big side. I was transferred to the sixth cottage. Bob transferred to the fifth cottage. Once transferred to sixth cottage, my interest in girls increased even though I was still on the small side. I traded my roller skates with a kid who had a sister on the girls' side.

In return, I was invited on his family visits to the girls' campus when they visited his sister. Now, I had treats and visits to the girl's campus. After joint visits, we went our separate ways until his next family visit. Our relationship was tied to our agreement. I made sure to find him on Sundays. Friendships made with girls transferred to the big side.

More and more, I looked forward to being transferred to the big side. Once assigned, I'd be eligible to be assigned to a position that paid a small stipend. The positions were few and in high demand. Having a little money would enable me to attend a movie or grab a hamburger in town. Bartering for cigarettes and clothes were other sources of income. Shop courses housed in the Trade School also offered a few opportunities to earn money.

Aunt Dolly!

Dad arrived with a new Aunt. We were told to call her Aunt Dolly. She complemented Dad's usual bag of chocolate kisses with fried chicken. The smell of fried chicken was overwhelming. Fried chicken and treats. Does it get better than that? Unbeknownst, we were participants in Dad acclimating and positioning us to accept Aunt Dolly as our mom. We were clueless. Really!

Dad and Aunt Dolly showed together. We showed up. They left. We retreated to games, friends, and obeying rules. Years passed. We were almost thinking for ourselves. Sort of 'testing the waters.' Dad and Aunt Dolly's visits were looked forward to, so long as fried chicken accompanied them.

Eventually, even with fried chicken, their twice a month visits lasting less than two hours couldn't compete against influences available to us at The Mount. We were transporting through our teenage years. Freedom, decision making, being on our own; Dad was less and less in demand.

An example was while I attended a movie on a Saturday in Tottenville, I missed Dad's visit. Not intentionally, just didn't think of it. Dad went nuts. Al and Bob received the third degree. I didn't care. Dad's influences were wearing thin.

"Mom" "Photos"

Dad arrived without Aunt Dolly and fried chicken. Nothing was said by us or Dad about her absence; which had developed into normal behavior for us. Before leaving us, Dad pulled out pictures of Mom! He handed us small black and white photos. Whoa! They were photos taken of Mom, with us. I was confused, again.

I kept staring at the photo with me and Mom. It's been several years since Mom was a part of our lives. A memory of 'The men in White' marching Mom through our apartment reappeared. Why was Dad giving us several small black and white photos of Mom? Was Mom OK? Dad said nothing. He didn't appear in any of the photos. We asked, "Where's Mom?" Up to this point we hadn't heard a single word from Dad about her. Or for that matter, not from relatives either. Not a single word!

Are we going to see Mom?
Dad mumbled, "She's gone."
Wow! Mom was gone. That was it. "Mom's gone."
Dad's words hit home. Dad got in his car, waved, and drove off. What the hell! We're standing in front of the quarantine, holding photos of Mom. He never mentioned Mom to us again. Ever! Dad's announcement, "Mom's gone" left us to grieve in our own way. We couldn't see Mom. We were under age. Was Dad kidding? Did he think all he had to do was tell us Mom was gone? That was enough to satisfy us? What the Hell! Black and white photos of Mom were all we were left with. Questioning Dad about Mom was useless. The day of reckoning was just around the corner.

Schooling

The Mount

Grammar school at The Mount was taught by the sisters of Saint Francis. High school was taught by priests and brothers. School at The Mount pretty much matched the Catholic schools we attended in Brooklyn with an exception. Girls at The Mount, housed in dormitories across Hyland Boulevard, were about a quarter mile away. I was placed in third grade. Sister Rose Assumpter was our teacher. Her teaching style was intimidating; a no-nonsense profile. I felt uncomfortable. I smiled. I completed work assignments on time. I joined kids asking questions; basically, my version of kissing up.

Sister Rose Assumpter emphasized arithmetic, addition, division, multiplication, and subtraction tables. She drilled them into us. We wrote and recited them daily. I know. I know. Arithmetic tables. Really! Today Mathematics seemingly are converted on a daily basis to new complex applications. At any rate, arithmetic, English, reading, and religious programs throughout grammar school years were handled by the sisters of Saint Francis as well as additional responsibilities; preparing kids for first communion and confirmation.

Sisters for the most part were pleasant, helpful, and approachable. Sisters like Sister Maureen, Sister Andrew, and Sister Jean Marie stood out. Sister Maureen was tall and soft-spoken. She taught fourth grade and religion classes. I recall her telling our class "When you're playing, always make sure to drink plenty of water. When you need energy, eat chocolate." I think she had a reason for imparting that information to us.

Sister Jean Marie was Mother Superior. She was responsible for administrative activities at The Mount. Her office was in the convent building. It was built on high ground overlooking the small and big side campuses. From time to time, Sister Jean Marie sent for me to plant flowers in front of the convent. We planted large colorful flowers spelling out the initials, M.I.V. (Mission of the Immaculate Virgin). To this day, M.I.P. appears in front of the convent. She made me feel good about myself. She was special.

Days before leaving The Mount, Sister showed me a cross, with Jesus crucified on the cross; similar to the ones worn by the sisters. She unscrewed a small knob from the bottom of the cross, revealing a very small item. "John, this is a special crucifix. This is a holy relic. I want you to have it." I've kept it throughout all the years. It has a special meaning for me; unexplainable. I keep it in a scarf given to me by Mom.

Mission of the Immaculate Virgin Mary Church

Our church was awesome. It was large, built of stone with high, towering twin peaks. All Masses and Holy Days of observation were strictly observed. Religious instructions were emphasized and taught by priests, sisters, and brothers. Services mirrored what we experienced at Saint Jerome and Saint Thomas Aquinas churches. A primary difference was the amount of obligatory services observed. Daily masses, Holy Days of Obligation Masses, High Masses; Wednesday evening Benedictions; you name it, The Mount had it.

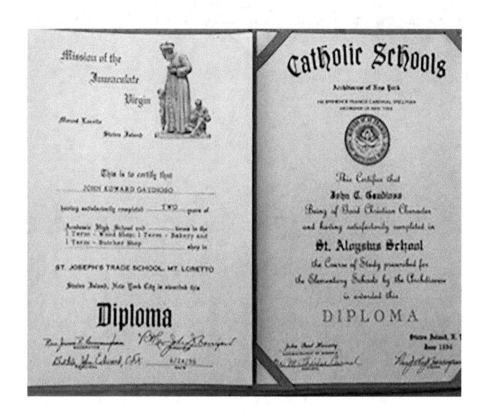

Diploma on the left has my name as
John Edward Gaudioso
On the right, it's John Christopher Gaudioso
WEIRD!

Transferred to the Big Side

Somewhere around my thirteen birthday, I was transferred to the big side. For me, it was a gigantic leap. Supervision lessened. We were assigned to buildings with large dormitories. We were supervised by lay staff, Xavier brothers and priests. The difference between the small side and the big side was immediate. Things got really interesting. Sports were played at a higher level. Saint Joseph's Trade School emphasized religious studies and trade opportunities; Tailoring, Wood working, Electrical, Printing, Butcher, and Bakery shops.

Once established on the big side, Al was transferred to the infirmary staff. He earned $2.50 a month. I got lucky. Well, sort of. I was placed in the butcher shop as a last resort. "I didn't perform well in previous trade shops. Whereas

Al was successfully competing in academics and trade school subjects. At any rate, the butcher shop paid $1.75 a month. I had money for a movie, candy, and bartering for things I needed. Bob wasn't assigned to a paying position. I'll assume he had passing grades.

The Mount featured a band. Kids practiced daily on one of the upper floors in the Trade School building. Musical sounds from instruments flowed throughout the trade building windows. I remember someone playing on a trumpet 'A Cherry Pink and Apple Blossom Time' tune. It sounded good. I wonder if he stayed with it.

One day I wandered into the band room for no particular reason other than being bored. Next thing I knew; I was blowing through a cornet horn. I couldn't hit a note for the life of me. Yet, I was accepted into the band. What a hoot!

The Mount Loretto Band marched in the Saint Patrick's Day parades. To my amazement, I was included. Sisters measured us for marching uniforms. We were bused to the parade grounds. I had my cornet. I was dressed in a matching uniform. Cool! I marched with the band, blowing through the damn Cornet, not even close to matching whatever the band was playing. I snuck looks at people clapping and cheering as we marched past them. I returned the horn to the band room. Cool!

Saint Joseph Trade School

Trade shop courses required an average of two years. Woodworking, printing, electrical, tailoring, butchering, bakery, and farming were offered. Students completing two years transferred to a public school in Tottenville to complete the remaining two years of high school.

Al excelled throughout Trade School. His success in Mr. Fisher's wood shop exposed him to hidden skills in woodworking. He was comfortable working with different types of natural colored woods. He built a secretary desk in 1956, bound together with glue and wooden dowels. He curved out wood bowls mixing in woods of different textures. Somehow, I've managed to store many of Al's handiwork throughout the years. My hope is to pass them on to family members.

He completed two years harnessing his wood working skills. He transferred to Tottenville high school where he would complete the last two years in high school.

Saint Joseph Trade school
Graduation, 1956
Al is in top row on the left
Brother Clyde, Fr. Cunningham,
Cardinal Corrigan, and Brother John

Al's recollections

Orientation at Tottenville High School began with a serious application of stereotyping. Students from The Mount were separated from students from neighboring homes. Being separated from other students made it clear that students from The Mount weren't viewed in the same light as students from neighboring areas. They weren't assigned to academic classes. Instead, they were assigned to trade shops. They were told they would be more comfortable. "Really!"

Additional Examples of Prejudice

Al was awarded for his woodworking skills. His teacher presented him with his award, a hammer. He told Al, "Don't hit anyone with it." Geez! Al frequented stores in Tottenville for small purchases. One of Al's hobbies was building model airplanes. He needed a piece of balsam wood. The salesman knew Al from previous purchases. He charged $1.00 for the balsam wood. A man nearby complained. Al wasn't charged tax. Al should be charged tax, just like everyone else. Al paid the 2 cents tax. The theatre in Tottenville had a rule. Boys from The Mount were assigned to a special section. Really!

Al was an avid stamp collector. He was a member of Jamestown Stamp Co. He was late on a monthly payment. He was notified that he was behind in his monthly membership subscription. Al was earning $2.50 a month. He over reacted. He discontinued his membership. He quit collecting stamps. He took his entire collection to a mailbox where he dumped his collection of stamps into it. "Don't upset Al."

My Turn

I had zero interest in academics. Being transferred to Trade School offered a welcome change. I was assigned to woodworking shop. Our instructor, Mr. Fisher was a small, thin man with glasses. He wore a white apron and smoked continuously throughout lecturing from his bench.

Al preceded me in Mr. Fisher's woodworking shop. Al took to woodworking like a bee to honey. He fashioned wooden candy bowls made with small wooden blocks with natural colors which enhanced the bowls. He completed projects well in advance of classmates. He was assigned to assist students with their projects. Al was a top-performing student in Mr. Fisher's wood shop class.

Mr. Fisher stood in front of our bench, smoking while explaining projects and his expectations from each of us. We were expected to complete three projects throughout the first semester. We were encouraged to work alone. But, in some cases, fellow students could provide assistance once they completed their projects.

Mr. Fisher explained our first project. He made smoking seem pleasurable, taking time between puffs, holding the cigarette between his fingers, speaking slowly, clearly, and eyeing students. Every once in a while, he paused, looking at me. Mr. Fisher figured out Al and I were brothers. I was doomed.

Did he wonder, *I hit the jackpot. John is Al's brother. Is he as talented as Al?*

OMG. I was super doomed. Mr. Fisher lectured on the use of tools and safety. He announced, we were going to build a game board. A game board! *Oh goody.*

Our assignment was to whittle a piece of wood to an eight-by-eight-inch square. Twenty-four holes in equal columns and spaced accordingly would be drilled into the game board. We were expected to complete the project within three weeks' time. Mr. Fisher excitedly presented a completed game board, built by a student. Al? The game board had marbles laid into the holes. Oh boy! That did it for me. I was excited!

Hand drills and saws were available. I set to work, determined to complete my project. I penciled an eight-by-eight-inch square on the piece of wood. I clamped it to the bench. I cut each side as close to the penciled lines as I could. The wood piece moved a few times. I tightened the clamp. It still moved. I continued sawing through square wood. In time, my wooden game board no longer measured to eight-by-eight inches.

I avoided Mr. Fisher. Eventually, as he made his way throughout the class inspecting game boards, he reached my position. Mr. Fisher stared at my game board. I smiled. He asked why I didn't request help. Minutes passed. I smiled. A few students around my position. There were laughs. Mr. Fisher wasn't amused. My game board wasn't square. In fact, it was short of the eight-by-eight-inch measurements by several inches. Geez!

I was assigned to a student to assist me. I'd keep the game board I had. I had to re-measure it into another square. I would drill as many holes as necessary equal to the new measurement of the game board. The kid assigned to me wasn't much help. He worked on his game board. I was left on my own. I tried. It wasn't meant to be. Eventually, my game board measured just short of five inches. I drilled a few holes. Two of them went through the wood. I was doomed.

Three weeks arrived. I stared at game boards displayed on a bench. Very impressive. How did they do that? My game board received snickers and laughs. Mr. Fisher, smoking a cigarette, reviewed the game boards. Surprisingly, my game board wasn't the only one incomplete. The difference was my game board didn't come close to resembling a game board. At least not the one Mr. Fisher had in mind.

He had a puzzled look as he reviewed my game board. If I could have read his mind? It would have been, *Is this guy really related to Al?* I was excused from the next class project. I was received a 'special project.' I was given a bowling ball pin. Mr. Fisher explained, I would convert the bowling ball pin into a lamp. The first step was to rasp the plastic cover from it. Each day, I rasped the plastic covering off the bowling ball pin. It was slow-going.

When some of the wood showed through, I was encouraged. I felt good about my 'special' project. Shaving off the covering with a metal rasp was slow and tedious. Mr. Fisher didn't seem concerned. I noticed boys using a lathe to shape wood. I had an idea. I asked a boy to attach my bowling ball pin to the lathe. He was hesitant. I bugged him. He attached the bowling ball pin to the lathe. He stood back. I hit the switch.

The bowling ball pin began spinning. I began shaving the cover from the spinning bowling ball pin. Shavings flew in all directions. Flames shot out from the spinning bowling ball pin. Boys backed off, yelling for Mr. Fisher. The bowling ball pin was on fire. He came running toward the flaming bowling ball. He turned off the switch. The lathe stopped spinning. He tossed sand from a bucket over the bowling ball, smothering out the fire. He stared at me. His face was beet red. I didn't have a good feeling! He carefully removed the 'torched' bowling ball pin from the lathe. He laid it down on his lecturing bench. He ordered all electrical equipment shut down. He ordered us to our bench.

He lit a cigarette, *to calm himself down?* He explained bowling ball pins were covered with a plastic coating. The spinning of the lathe caused the plastic to catch on fire. Mr. Fisher was upset with me. For the remainder of the week, I was assigned to sweeping clippings and wood shavings from work areas.

A few days later, Mr. Fisher escorted me to the administration office. He spoke with the administrator, a Xavier Brother, for a few minutes before turning and, without a word, walked out of the office. I remained standing. Brother shuffled papers. He was on the phone with someone. Dad? That would have been interesting. He laid down the phone. "John, I'm transferring you to the electrical shop class."

Following a pep talk, I was escorted to the electrical shop class. A second chance at a new career. The electrical shop instructor barely acknowledged me. I don't remember his name. He seemed nervous. I wondered if Mr. Fisher filled

159

him in on me. The instructor mumbled that I wouldn't receive credit for missed class projects. I would receive credit for passing any remaining projects.

I joined my new classmates on a bench facing the instructor. He proceeded to explain how a battery causes a light bulb to light up. I already knew the answer. I yelled out, "A light switch." This course was going to be a breeze. The instructor stared at me – for a long time. He advised me to not shout out. I needed to raise my hand when I had questions and answers. And, by the way, he informed the class there was more to lighting a bulb than by flipping a switch. Geez!

He held up red and white wires. He explained the differences between them. Red was positive. White was negative. One ends of the corresponding wires were connected to corresponding terminals on a battery. The other ends of the wires were connected to corresponding terminals on box with a light bulb attached to it. When a knob on the light box was turned, electricity would flow from the battery terminals to the light bulb terminals, causing the light bulb to light up. Boys were taking down notes. Notes! I didn't even have paper or a pencil. No one told me I had to take notes.

The instructor reviewed the process a few times. We took turns connecting wires and turning knobs. I was on my way to becoming an electrician. My time spent in the electrical shop was interesting. However, by missing out on previous projects and not being able to complete them, I was assigned to observing and assisting classmates on remaining projects. The bottom line: I managed to come away with incomplete grades in woodworking and electrical shops. Options, please?

Another meeting with administration! My options were limited. It was either the printing shop or the tailor shop. Brother made a few calls, again, on my behalf. He placed the phone down. He looked me straight in the eye. You are assigned to the printing shop through the last semester. I had no idea there were so many options available.

The printing shop was located in another building, not far from Saint Joseph's Trade School. I liked the printing shop class almost immediately. Boys, in aprons were busily doing 'printing stuff.' My third instructor, explained the purpose of the shop. We were responsible for printing flyers with messages. Advancements within the shop were based on performance.

I was assigned to printing flyers, using the Pattern Printing Press. I arranged lead letters onto a message board. Black ink was applied to a round iron surface. The message board with lead spelled words was lowered onto an inked surface; then was pressed onto the flyer. It was a fun assignment. Didn't Ben Franklin run a printing press shop?

In time, I was transferred to an area as a 'type setter.' I learned to set type into wooden cribs, which held the type in place. Before releasing the crib for printing, I learned to read the type printed copy upside down. This assured spotting misspellings more easily. Duh!

Everything was moving along nicely. That is, until I was contacted by a few older boys. They melted the lead letters in coffee containers. The melted lead was shaped into small round oval pieces, used in fistfights. These guys were serious. I foolishly agreed to remove lead letters from the printing shop. In time the discovery of missing lead letters was noted. I came under suspicion. Did I know anything about the missing lead letters? I replied, "No." Even though I wasn't accused of removing the lead letters, I was reassigned to printing flyers off the pattern-printing press.

There weren't more reports of missing lead letters? That may have had something to do with my receiving an unsatisfactory grade in printing shop.

I managed to finish out the semester. I looked forward to reporting to the print shop in the following school year. Following a few days into the summer break, I was summoned to report to administration. On the way to the office, I was hoping to be reassigned to the print shop. Admittedly I didn't set the world on fire in woodworking and electrical shops. As for printing shop, aside from being suspected of removing lead letters, my performance was satisfactory. Duh!

Butcher Shop

Brother looked up from his desk. He smiled. "Sit down, John. John, you need to get yourself together. I'm giving you one last chance. I'm assigning you to the butcher shop. It's a temporary assignment, lasting through the summer."

I must have shot him a blank look. He continued, "You report tomorrow. You'll be evaluated at the end of the summer. If your performance is good, you'll be assigned to a permanent position in the butcher shop. If your performance is not up to expectations, you'll be assigned to the tailor shop. The tailor shop is the last opportunity for you. Fail it and you're going to repeat the year. You will be paid $1.75 cents a month." Really! I was going to earn money? I knew Al was earning $2.50 a month working in the infirmary. Being paid was a good thing. Besides, I was running out of options

Mr. Mulligan

I reported for work. Three of us were assigned to the butcher shop. Two were permanently assigned. Mr. Mulligan introduced himself to me. He told me that I was assigned to work with them throughout the summer. If things worked out, I would be transferred to the shop on a permanent basis. He didn't mention my previous workshop experiences though I'm certain he was briefed. I was thankful for that. Another big side plus: we weren't required to attend Sunday suppers. I usually 'attended' a movie in Tottenville, followed by a Sunday supper. I'd ordered burger and coke. I had enough money for my supper. Mom would have been proud.

Mr. Mulligan's mannerisms were, matter of fact, down to earth. He was friendly enough, mixed into being someone who wouldn't put up with nonsense. Initially, he worked closely with me, supervising my introduction into butchering. Within a few weeks, he surprised me. I was permanently assigned to the butcher shop.

Occasionally we were left to ourselves when working on our butcher blocks. Other times, we'd assist with unloading supplies from the dock. One of the men working the docks always gave us a rough time, just for the hell of it. He was a strange one!

The immediate difference between Mr. Mulligan and my previous teachers was that he was approachable. He emphasized everyone worked as a team. Mr. Mulligan worked on a long steel table facing our cutting blocks. He kept an eye on us as we performed or duties. His specialty were special cuts of meats and fish, destined for the dining tables of priests, nuns, brothers, and lay personnel. When not butchering, Mr. Mulligan's unbuttoned white apron swung as he walked throughout the kitchen and dock area.

Once we were all pretty much into routines, Mr. Mulligan relaxed. He often spoke about his son who was employed as a crewmember on merchant marine ships. He shared photos of places his son visited while docked in ports throughout the world. He didn't mention a wife. He was a quiet man. He never raised his voice. He was a good teacher.

He explained the different ways of handling very sharp knives. Meats required cross cuts; trimming fat required leaving just enough fat to flavor the meats as they cooked. When gutting chickens, smaller knifes were used for close work. Even when we were well-versed in using the knives, he'd always begin each process verbally cautioning us about the type and use of the knives.

The shop housed a very large freezer. Fish, chickens, and other assorted meats were stored alongside of hindquarters, hanging from hooks. Mr. Mulligan was the only one strong enough to place and remove large hindquarters from the hooks. He let us prepare Kool-Aid and stored the jugs inside the freezer. On hot summer days we took swigs from the jugs.

Mr. Mulligan shared with us exactly what we needed to know related to our responsibilities. I was comfortable, no pressure. We reported to work at 7 am five days a week. We worked through 12 noon, Monday through Fridays. Afternoons were a free time for us in summer months. School was attended in afternoons throughout winter months. O occasions, based on the needs of the kitchen, one or two of us would assist Mr. Mulligan with whatever had to be done. Earning $1.75 cents a month was an incentive. My attitude improved. I was learning a skill, and surprisingly, enjoying it

Mr. Mulligan worked alongside us, offering us breaks as we needed them. The exception being chickens. He left them to us. He worked at his own block, trimming special cuts or preparing fish. Fish was an area only he could handle. It was slippery, heavy to handle, and, at times, carrying an overwhelming odor. Mr. Mulligan's apron was always crispy clean at the start of his workday. By the end, it was covered with blood, guts, and other stuff.

Stew Meat

Our primary responsibility was trimming beef, gutting chickens, and maintaining a clean working area. Other responsibilities required us to assist Mr. Mulligan when called on. We could always count on assisting him, when he needed to pull down a hindquarter from a hook. He'd grab hold of the hindquarter, lifting it up and over the hook. Once stabilizing it, he stumbled forward through the open freezer door, half tossing and half leaning his body into his cutting table. He'd rest the hindquarter on the table. It was difficult for him. But, he managed it.

Once the hindquarter was in position, He'd begin cutting slabs of beef, which he distributed to us. We removed excess fat from the beef which was the first. Leaving a small amount of fat was important as fat added favor to the cooked stew. Once trimmed, we cut the beef into small squares. The process was easy enough, once we were into our grooves. The cut stew meat pieces were deposited into pails, placed at our cutting blocks. Full pails were unloaded by kitchen staff into large cylinder pots used for cooking.

Gutting Chickens

We gutted hundreds of chickens weekly. The chickens were delivered to the receiving dock weekly. They were semi-frozen, packed in chipped ice in wooden crates. We'd assist the deliveryman in unloading the crates of chickens from the truck into the shop. He was a nice guy. He gave us a few coins for helping him unload the truck.

Once unloaded, we set crates alongside our chopping blocks. Knives were distributed. Waste barrels and bowls of cold water were situated nearby. The cold water was for dipping semi-frozen fingers into the water to reduce the pain in our fingers, caused by inserting them deep into the cavity of semi-frozen chickens.

Gutting chickens was a nasty process. A peculiar foul odor rose from the crates as the lids were removed. The feathers, chicken heads, and legs were removed. Gutting began with a deep cut alongside the neck of the chicken. The crop bag was removed. Often it contained undigested food, saved for a late-night snack? The crop bag was tossed into the waste bin.

With the chicken flat on its back, I'd make an incision completely around the butt. It was added to the waste bin. I'd enter the cavity with my hand, securing the row of undeveloped eggs, ranging in size from tiniest to a full-size egg. Full-sized eggs were carefully removed and put aside for Mr. Mulligan.

Reinserting frozen fingers deep into the cavity to remove lungs from both sides caused fingers to become almost frozen. Once removed, my fingers were again inserted to remove the stomach, intestines, and heart. All were tossed into the waste bin. The gutted chicken was tossed into large rising water tanks where they were flushed with continuous running water. Once rinsed the chickens were transferred to the kitchens where they would be prepared for supper, feeding hundreds of boys and girls, including the administrative staff, priests, counselors, brothers, and nuns.

Chicken George

We worked with a boy named George. He was very funny, mischievous, sometimes bordering on wild. His antics kept us in stitches. You never knew what to expect from George. However, he excelled in butchering. Mr. Mulligan placed him in charge whenever he grabbed a smoke or was needed on the dock. When we were gutting chickens, as normal, we fell into a 'quiet zone.' We ignored each other. We needed to focus on our task. We were working with very sharp knives. We paid attention to the work at hand. On one of those occasions Mr. Mulligan stepped out for a smoke break, leaving George to monitor us as we gutted chickens.

I was in a zone: into cutting, gutting, removing unused innards from chicken cavities, when, in the corner of my eye, I caught a glimpse of George removing a chicken from the rinsing tank. This was unusual. Once tossed into the rinsing tank, chickens remained there to run through a wash cycle before being removed.

George noticed me looking toward him. He lifted a chicken from the water, laughing. He had my attention. I laid down my knives. He was looking over the chicken. He submerged it into the water again before taking it out of the water. George tucked the chicken under his soiled blooded apron. I alerted the other kid. We realized what George had in mind. We yelled for George to put the chicken back in the water.

George ran behind Mr. Mulligan's butchering table, laughing as we continued yelling for him to put the chicken back in the rinsing tank. He kept his distance from us. If Mr. Milligan popped back into the shop – we'd all be fired. George tucked the dead chicken under his apron. Oh no! His apron was popping in and out like a jackhammer. We were laughing and shouting at the same time, telling George to stop. George leaned against the tile wall. The chicken's small wings were flipping from the opening of his apron.

There was no stopping him. We pleaded with George to stop. Finally, he pulled the limp and lifeless chicken from his apron and turned toward the rinsing tank. We yelled. "Not the rinsing tank, George." He held the chicken over his head. George tossed the raped chicken into the rinsing tank. The chicken disappeared, mixing in with other chicken carcasses.

We wanted to kill George! He resumed his position at his cutting block, laughing while gutting chickens. We didn't retrieve the chicken. Duh! Chicken was served for supper that night. We were pissed. We cursed George up and down. George laughed. George was one sick puppy. Oh, I ate chicken that night.

George Again!

The freezer housed meats, hindquarters, fish, chickens, and a water jug of Kool-Aid were stored in a large walk-in freezer. The huge hindquarters hanging from hooks were too heavy for us to lift individually. Even Mr. Mulligan struggled removing a hindquarter off the hook. He had us hold open the freezer door. He grappled with the hindquarter, walking unsteadily, out of the freezer and, slamming the hindquarter down on a dolly.

Another time, while he was taking a smoke break, we retreated into the freezer for drinks of Kool-Aid from the water jug. George wandered over to where several hindquarters hung from hooks. He selected the smallest hindquarter; George lifted it off the hook. He started doing a crazy dance, trying to balance himself, while holding on to the hindquarter. George was stumbling, calling us to help him. We were laughing our butts off. We didn't move. We just laughed, bending over and laughing at George who was clearly in trouble. He half fell to the floor, releasing the hindquarter at the same time. We were in stitches.

George was up, attempting to lift the hindquarter as he begged us to help him. We had no choice. Mr. Mulligan would be upset with all of us, not just George. We surrounded the hindquarter. We wrapped our arms and hands around ice-cold frozen meat, attempting to grip it. We lifted it up, someone laughed. We dropped the hindquarter. George was laughing in spite of begging us to lift the hindquarter onto the table. We tried again and again. We were useless. Besides, it was too heavy and slippery.

The freezer door opened. We backed up from the hindquarter which was lying on the freezer floor. Without a word Mr. Mulligan retrieved a meat hook. He stuck it deep into the hindquarter. We assisted him as he pulled on the hook. Once the hindquarter was upright, he said. "Get your butts ready to lift the damned thing, when I say so." We got the hindquarter hooked up.

Mr. Mulligan was upset. He didn't ask how the hindquarter came off the hook. He mumbled something to the effect, "It better not happen again." He headed for the dock, most likely to grab a smoke and, calm down. George was a piece of work.

Responsibilities involved cleaning work areas; a must-do chore after each day's work. Floors were swept clean, scraps were gathered and scraped into a large waste bin. Mr. Mulligan inspected the floors, wall tiles, and the large steel water sinks. We finished the day, hosing down tile walls and floors. The water flowed into drainage grids installed in the floor. Needless to say, every so often we got carried away with hosing tile walls and floor areas. Someone splashing too close to someone else was justification for watering each other as completely as we could.

Mr. Mulligan was outside on the dock, smoking, and talking with fellow dock staff. Hey! After cleaning chickens, our aprons, pants, and sneakers were coated with chicken guts and blood. We smelled really bad. Watering was welcomed. Eventually, Mr. Mulligan yelled in from the dock area, "That's enough in there. Let's close it up." My feeling was that Mr. Mulligan enjoyed our group. We performed well as a group. He trusted us. He gave us latitude. He understood us!

Bakery Shop

I finished out summer, completing another school semester and a stint in the butcher shop where I was paid $1.75 a month. I got lucky. Transferred to the Bakery Shop. I'm certain Mr. Mulligan vouched for me. My earnings working in the bakery shop would pay me $2.25 per month, an increase of 50 cents. George was assigned to one of the workshops in the trade school. If George was transferred to the bakery shop, there's no telling what he would have done with a warm loaf of fresh baked bread!

I reported to Mr. Ryan. An apartment for him and his family was provided on the girl's side of The Mount. He definitely was not approachable or as friendly as Mr. Mulligan. He was high strung; with off-handed comments. Still, having worked for Mr. Mulligan in the butcher shop worked in my favor. The bakery shop was the same as the butcher shop as far as the location and small staff were concerned. Now, I was kneading dough for bread and rolls, prepared daily or the boys, girls, and staff personnel.

Another kid was assigned to the bakery shop with me. Mr. Ryan met us on our first day. He didn't bother with formalities. We were transfers. We joined join two kids who were retained from the previous year. Mr. Ryan explained responsibilities and expectations of what was to be done and expected of us.

We baked enough bread and rolls five days a week, to be available through a weekend. An exception are Wednesdays when baked rolls are served with cooked rice for supper. Buns. If additional bread was needed, we baked beyond Friday.

We understood our responsibilities. Early each morning, Mr. Ryan greeted us as we sleep-walked through the bakery doors for work. The huge baking ovens were fired up. Ovens were checked repeatedly, assuring the desired temperature was on target. Once satisfied, Mr. Ryan measured ingredients of flour, water, sugar, and yeast into a large steel mixing vat. When the dough was ready to be removed from the vat, we settled into positions around the table which was floured.

Mr. Ryan pulled dough from the vat, weighing the first pieces for the proper weight and texture of the dough. He was fast and accurate, cutting dough into perfect pieces and rolling them on the table. We reached the dough, rolling the dough into loafs for bread or rolls. The rolled dough were placed into large baking trays.

Once satisfied the ovens were at the proper temperature, Mr. Ryan placed each of the trays into the rotating oven shelves. He removed each tray from the ovens and placed on racks to cool down. Kitchen staff removed the cooled racks of bread or rolls into a storage area in the large kitchen.

Inventory

A part of our responsibilities required us to transfer arriving inventory from the docks into storage rooms. We were supervised by the dock staff who were adults. Inventoried goods were kept under lock and key. They checked in the inventory. We loaded it onto dollies and transferred the inventory. Goods arriving were delivered in bulk; sacks of flour, sugar, large milk containers, jars of jelly, mustard, ketchup, and canned goods to name a few items.

Taking a Risk!

We were determined to steal whatever we could, past the eyes of the dock staff. It wasn't easy. We were watched closely. There was one dock man; a heavy smoker, thin as a rail, and ornery as all-get-out. He was noted for turning in boys who were caught removing inventory from the kitchen areas. In the past, boys caught removing stored goods from the storage rooms were usually transferred back to one of the trade shops. With few opportunities and keeping the whereabouts of dock workers, in particular the one who was noted for looking to catch us removing goods from the storage rooms.

Nevertheless, we were determined to remove food items. We developed a workable plan. Assigned to the bakery, we had to restock the heavy sacks of flour and sugar for baking. Mr. Ryan didn't hang around once we were in the last stages of cleaning up. He left. We were unsupervised. But not for long. We approached the dock man, explaining, we needed to pull out sacks of flour and sugar for next day's baking. He complained as he always did before unlocking the storage room door. He was lazy. A plus in our favor was that Mr. Ryan expected his supplies to be on hand for baking when he arrived in the morning.

Once the inventory was ready to transferred, we assisted each other transferring the heavy slacks of flour and sugar, resting every few steps, complaining of the weight. The dock man noticed. He'd yell at us to move our asses. We continued complaining as we transferred the sacks of flour and sugar. He followed us as we exited the storage room. He enjoyed seeing us struggling. A few laughs before yelling "You better be finished before I come back." He walked out to the dock area for a smoke.

We made quick work clearing the sacks from the dolly; and returning for a second supply. We needed to be fast. We hid jars of jelly, sacks of cookies, anything that could be hidden between sacks of flour and sugar. It was a small window of opportunity. We raced to the bakery shop. We hid everything in and around, pots, pans, and slack of flour and sugar. We returned the empty dolly back to the storage room. "Mister, we're finished." He emerged from the dock, muttering to himself.

He yelled; "Go on; scram!" We scrammed back to our dormitories.

Bartering

The Mount was no different from bartering in my old neighborhood in Brooklyn. We were a close group, representing the butcher and bakery shops. We agreed to share whatever we took from the storage room between us before bartering on campus.

Some shared items never reached the campus. We reheated the ovens. We warmed up bread or buns and cooked beef burgers. Loafs of warm bread sliced lengthwise, filled with meats or jelly was worth the chances we took. Bartering on campus was small time. It involved little risk. Whatever was bartered or traded for was the first of multi trades throughout the campus. The penalty, if caught, guaranteed being returned to the trade school and enrolled one of the shops. Assignment to campus was automatic.

When a boy needed something I didn't have, I'd reach out to someone who had the item. We'd work out a three-way deal. Jeans, pink or black shirts, sneakers, shoes and belts were in demand. Most trades were permanent. Some boys rented out things needed for dances, movies, or a visit off campus. Everything was negotiable.

Poison Ivy

Bob spent time exploring in the nearby woods. While exploring, he came in contact with poison ivy which grew throughout the surrounding woods. At any rate, Bob caught a very serious case of poison ivy. A counselor spotted Bob wandering on campus grounds. He was shocked to discover Bob covered with poison ivy. He escorted him to the infirmary.

The poison ivy spread rapidly throughout his body. His face was so swollen, he had to drink through a straw. His eyes were mere slits; ears, lips, neck, you name it; he was completely covered with poison ivy. Generous amounts of Calamine lotion were applied to his entire body. Bob was a walking carrot. One of the Bother's commented Bob had the most serious case of poison ivy he'd ever seen.

Farming,
Barno's and Bob

Farming was introduced to The Mount in its early years. In time, the farm animals were reduced to cows, bulls and a few pigs. Boys assigned to their care were referred to as Barno's. They were older, stronger, and able to handle the responsibilities in maintaining a farm. They were housed separately near the farm. They didn't require close supervision. They kept to themselves. They were up at the crack of dawn milking cows, mucking stalls, and feeding live stock. The farm was located in the upper area campus, away from the campus cottages and schools. Occasionally, the smell of farm animals blew throughout the lower campus buildings.

Bob Meets Bull

Back to Bob. Following his recovery, Bob didn't return to the wooded areas. Duh. He continued wandering throughout the campus grounds. Eventually, he wandered into the farm. Barno's let him hang around. Gradually, Bob was given small jobs. Mucking out stalls was something he enjoyed. Really! While mucking out a stall, Bob noticed a cow being transferred from an adjoining stall into the one he was mucking out. Not a problem!

He'd been told how to protect himself from kicks from cows. A kick could be harmful. He knew to position himself to the side of a cow. He also knew in order for a cow to move, he needed to slap the cow hard on its rump. With a cow sharing the stall with Bob, he didn't think twice. He gave the cow a hard slap on its rump. Actually, it wasn't a cow. It was a bull. A big ugly black bull. It became agitated by Bob's slap to its rump.

It turned its massive head toward Bob. Bob was looking for a cow. He realized he was sharing the stall with a not-so friendly bull. He also realized he slapped the bull on his rump. Not a good thing! To his astonishment, the bull turned away from him. Being slapped by the smallest Barno ever most likely amused the bull. It stepped out of the stall into the open area.

Barno's noticed the bull emerging from the stall and rushed to steer the bull back into the stall. They were surprised to see Bob emerging from the stall, running for cover as they were steering back into the stall. In a way, it was Bob's baptism of fire. Bob changed his underwear.

Fighting

Fighting with kids on the small side carried over to the big side. While I had my share of fights, I avoided. I tried settling for a good argument which saved me many times from fighting. When neither of us backed off; well then, we fought. Once, while in line leaving the dining hall, I spotted a boy in line behind Al. He began making fun of Al. I caught his attention. I told him Al was my brother. He laughed. We got into it. One thing led to another. Before you knew it, we were on our way to the coal bins, not far from the dining hall, to fight.

As we walked to the area where the coal bins were, I recognized him. He shared his visits with me when he received a visit from his grandmother. We were friends. Once we were transferred to the big side, our friendships made on the small side was replaced by new friendships. I wasn't sure if he recognized me? Now, I didn't want to fight him. It was too late. We were encouraged by boys who were always up for a fight.

At the coal bins, we squared off, shuffling in and around each other. I looked into his eyes. I saw something. Maybe he did recognize me? I thought he'd back off and apologize. He didn't. I let go with a wild swing, catching him off guard, flush on his temple. He wheeled backward. He was surprised; so was I. His face flushed deep red. I backed off, expecting his response. He didn't seem to be in a hurry. Boys jeered, cheered, and continued encouraging us to fight.

"Chicky, chicky," a familiar call known to all. Someone in authority was coming our way. We scattered in all directions. I spotted the reason for the alert. I recognized the Sister coming toward us. She was waving her arms, shouting for us to stop running. It was a Sister who, from time to time, was assigned to supervise our work areas. She was Sister Coconut. She rewarded boys with coconut cookies when they completed their work.

I followed boys to the gymnasium. He was already there. I wasn't looking for a resumption of our fight. I walked toward him. "Are we finished?"

He mumbled, "Yeah," turned, and walked away. I felt bad about the fight. We never hooked up again.

Once, while looking out a window of the trade school building, actually daydreaming, I noticed two boys getting ready to fight. The fight didn't last very long. The smaller boy was super-fast. His punches into the taller boy's stomach caused him to drop to his knees. He was sucking for air, but, struggled to his feet. The smaller boy again rushed him, pounding both fists into his stomach. Again, the boy dropped. He struggled getting up, clearly out of breath. He stood up and waved the boy off. They shook hands. It was over. I was impressed with how the smaller boy handled himself.

Another time, I got into an argument with a boy. He said some things to me; I can't recall the specifics. He ran off. I chased after him. He headed into the wooded area behind the Trade School. I was closing the gap between us. He reached and crossed a small pond which was frozen over. I followed him. Duh!

I could hear ice cracking under my feet. I tried turning back for the shore. It was too late. I plunged me into icy water up to my waist. The boy was already on the other shore. He turned looking at me. We stared at each other. He was laughing. I bend over the ice to lift myself out of the icy cold water. My gonads were freezing. I wasn't getting anywhere. Without a word, he removed his jacket; and tossed it to me. I grabbed one of the sleeves. He pulled me out of the freezing water. We sat on the edge of the pond. He lit up a cigarette. We shared the butt.

Water Rats

On a hot summer day, a few of us headed to a beach area where Tottenville summer cabins were located. We stayed close to surrounding wooded areas. We wanted to avoid being seen by anyone living in nearby cabins. We stripped down to swimming trunks or underwear and hid our clothes in the nearby shrubbery. Once in the water, we swam to a rowboat anchored about sixty feet from the shore.

It wasn't long before we heard shouts from several people, yelling for us to get out of the water. I spotted Father Pavis and counselors joining with them, yelling for us to get out of the water. Someone called The Mount. One by one, boys swam back to the shore. They gathered their clothes and were taken back to The Mount. I didn't swim back to the shore with the others. I managed to get on the other side of the rowboat. Several minutes passed. I peeked over the rail. There wasn't anyone on the beach. I shoved off from the rowboat, intending to swim back to the shore.

I soon realized I was drifting away from the rowboat and beach. The tide was drifting me out further to the ocean. I swam as hard as I could to regain my grip on the rowboat. I rested before deciding to swim for the shore as fast and with everything I had to the shore. Once there, I raced for the shrubbery where my clothes were hidden.

Nothing! They were gone. A not so funny feeling embraced me. I hightailed it back to The Mount, keeping as close to the wooden areas as possible. I emerged from the woods in my wet swim trunks, or in my underwear? Can't remember! I managed to sneak into my dormitory room where I changed into clothes. Word had gotten out, about boys caught swimming in Tottenville beach – which was off limits to us.

I was concerned Father Pavis figured out whom the extra pair of clothes belonged to. I decided to own up. I knocked on Father Pavis's room. He shouted, "Come in." I did. "So, it's you, Gaudi." Father Pavis smiled from behind his desk. He pointed to my pile of clothes off in the corner of the room. He talked me through the dangers of swimming in the ocean. He repeated, the beach was off limits. He decided to give me a few slaps on my butt with a thick leather strap, he had on his desk. At supper, I was introduced along with my fellow swimmers to the entire dining hall as 'the Water Rats of Tottenville Beach.' Geez! Aside from a few whacks on my butt, I was in better shape than the other boys. Based on my position in the butcher shop, I was excused from serving campus time.

Payback!

I was being hassled by a group of boys. At first, I couldn't figure out why. I didn't know them. After repeated run-ins I recognized why I was being hassled. My run in the small side dining hall caught up with me. The boy who tried to starve me to death was hanging with the boys who were hassling me. I got it. He was still pissed.

He hung out with a tough group. I took the high road. It wasn't long before I ran into them in the dormitory. Someone grabbed me from behind. A small penknife blade was thrust into my back. It barely penetrated my jacket. I struggled. They had a good laugh. They had my attention.

A friend of mine, Fink. He was a loner. He was avoided. He didn't talk much, to anyone, including me. The one time he did, he was looking for a few cigarettes. He had nothing to trade or to pay with. It was an opportunity. I gave Fink a few cigarettes then and a few whenever I could. "No charge!" Duh! We got along. I happened to let him know, I was being hassled. He asked where they hung out. I told him, they usually hung out in the dorm dayroom after supper. Fink said he might drop in.

Dorm dayrooms, especially at night, attracted boys, mostly listening to the latest sounds from a radio station. Some played cards, others horsed around. No one bothered anyone. As usual, the kid with his group showed up. I was sitting across from them. As always, a few stares from them were coming in my direction. Before anything could happen. Fink walked into the dorm dayroom. He didn't waste time asking, "Is he here?" The group dispersed, leaving 'the boy' standing alone. It didn't matter that Fink was shorter than him. Fink was built like a fire hydrant. He was tough. No one, ever, messed with him.

He went directly to the boy. Fink's hand flew out so fast, he boy never knew what hit him. The room went quiet. The boy staggered back against the wall. He started to say something. Fink let loose with another swing, connecting with the boy's head, slamming it against the wall. He dropped.

He steadied himself in a kneeling position, looking up at Fink. His face was swelling up. He didn't move. Fink bent to say a few words to him. The boy was nodding in agreement. Fink walked toward me; gave me a friendly shove, smiled, and walked out of the dorm dayroom. There just aren't enough Finks in the world! I made sure to put aside a few extra butts for Fink.

Basketball

When I did play basketball, mostly on the small side; later on the big side, I was able to make up for being short by being very fast. I played with the house league basketball team. Our coach, 'Doc,' was soft spoken and easy-going. He emphasized playing according to positions. His drills repeated our positions over and over until we had them down pat.

Doc didn't bother with complicated plays. He emphasized taking advantage of rebounds and having players positioned to run and pass down court for scoring opportunities. As a team, we were known for shooting underhand from the foul line. Doc had us shooting from the foul line; underhand.

I was mostly positioned playing in a forward position. Doc team me with another player who was as fast as me. We were teamed together. We both had decent lay-up shots from either side of the net. We were alert to receiving rebounded basketballs. We split apart as we raced down the court in tandem, trading passes until one of us had a lay-up shot. It was fun.

There was another kid with the name Ray. Ray was the fastest kid on our team. He was also our best shooter, hitting from anywhere within his reach from the field. He was the difference in our wins. Once transferred to the big side, I played basketball in makeup games.

Football

I played on our in-house football team. For reasons unknown to this day, I was transferred to the travel team. It could have been due to them not having enough players? We wore white and green uniforms. I liked the colors. Coaches for the travel team had practice with the house team. They were competitive. They were winning games against home teams which wasn't difficult.

It turned out, travel team coaches were hell bent on qualifying for a tournament invite. After winning enough games, they qualified for a tournament invitation. The coaches were excited. They reemphasized practice drills. What were they thinking? We'd be playing in host state, Pennsylvania. Coaches emphasized drills over and over again. We were told teams playing in the tournament were beatable. This was a big deal.

On the day of departure for Pennsylvania, the priests, brothers, sisters, counselors, and Mount boys wished us good luck as we climbed aboard our busses. We were excited. Everyone was excited.

We arrived in Pennsylvania. Our bus parked next to other busses. Players departed busses, carrying equipment to a large building near the football stadium. Not far behind them were fans and families encouraging them on to victory. We unloaded our equipment. Players from other team were smiling, laughing, seemingly unconcerned as they entered the gymnasium to change into their uniforms.

I became concerned when our white and green uniforms attracted a few looks and laughs from members of other teams changing into their uniforms. Coaches hustled their players to dress into their uniforms. It became obvious, our team was on the small size. We were aware of stares looking in our direction. Were we doomed? We'd soon find out.

Over-Matched

Our coaches lined us up just inside the entrance to the stadium. They were encouraging; telling us we were ready. "The Mount Loretto football team" was announced over speakers to a packed stadium with fans. We ran onto the field. Fans and families cheered loudly as we took positions along the bench. Our names and numbers were announced. It was a cool moment.

The team we were playing was announced and were cheered as loudly as we were. The difference was when they were introduced by their name and number, their families and friends roared with each introduction. I realized our families and friends were nowhere to be heard. We had our coaches, period. Nevertheless, we were goosed; ready to mix it up.

The opening kickoff to our team was encouraging; for the other team. Our player was crushed as he coughed up the football. We couldn't defend against their players. Did I mention their players were tall and big? Their offensive line scored quickly and consistently throughout the game. We yielded first downs in buckets. They had their way with us defensively and offensively. It became obvious we were in for a very long day.

I wonder if our coaches were aware of what we would be up against. Football throughout Pennsylvania is a sacred ritual. Kids received their first football at the time of their birth. Then for the rest of their lives, they played, they ate, they slept, and dreamed football. Duh!

Our team tried hard. We applied what we were taught. We didn't give up. We just weren't competitive. We were in deep doo-doo throughout the entire game. Coaches moved us in and out of the game as often as possible. They needed to keep us involved. How about keeping us alive!

I was on the bench watching our opponent having their way with us. I heard my name over the loudspeaker. "Gaudioso with the tackle." Again, "Gaudioso with the tackle!" I was having a hell of a game. A player from our team was having a great game. And, I'm receiving credit for them. Cool! It gets better. An article featured my name in local newspapers. Son of a gun.

Mount Loretto Travel Teams

Aside from our disappointing performance, The Mount's varsity travel teams fielded competitive teams in a number of sports, Golden Gloves Boxing tournaments, Basketball, Baseball, and Football to name a few. Our varsity football players looked like giants. The varsity teams fielded talented big tough kids, mostly from the Barno's group. The Football team produced countless victories for The Mount.

Girls

Once transferred to the big side, girls were easier to meet. Previous friendships carried over from the small side enabled introductions between boys and girls. I was able to visit the girl's side without supervision. Not that there wasn't supervision, it wasn't enforced as strictly as it was on the small side. Another plus was working in the butcher and bakery shops. I was paid seventy-five cents a month. Additional money came from bartering and loaning out clothes, including shoes. I had money. I had clothes. I had jeans, shirt, and sneakers. Most importantly I was being introduced to independence.

Friday Night Dances

Friday night dances were restricted to the big side. Everyone attending scrambled for clothing. I had clean jeans, shirts, mostly pink and black, my favorite colors. I had shoes which were in demand. Owning shoes were a must when dancing. Sneakers weren't encouraged.

Preparations for Friday night dances began days in advance. Frenzied bartering for jeans, shirts, and shoes were the norm. White shirts were died black in sinks. Boys practiced the Lindy in dormitory games rooms and in the trade school bathrooms. Duck tails hair, combed back, was held in place by generous amounts of Vaseline or Dickey Peach gel. Belts featuring car emblems were popular. Boys on weekend visits to neighborhoods ripped emblems from cars. Cadillac emblems were highly prized.

I made certain to wear clean jeans, complete with a large belt buckle, a metal trademark logo removed from a Ford or Chevy by someone on leave from The Mount. My shirt, normally black, was swapped out for a tangerine colored shirt. My shoes were mine. We must have been quite a sight.

Dipping and Smoking

Sisters and counselors broke up couples caught dipping while dancing with a girl. It was taboo. More than one incident resulted in being banned from a future Friday night dance. Being successful dipping, a girl provided bragging rights. Geez!

Smoking wasn't permitted at Friday night dances. Smokers, older boys used bathrooms to sneak in a smoke. They opened windows, left bathrooms doors open and 'lit 'em up.' Spotters sounded "Chicky, Chicky," alerting smokers that counselors were headed toward the bathrooms. Smokers cleared out from bathrooms often passing counselors on their way to the bathrooms. Once entering a bathroom, counselors could be heard coughing. Fun!

Last Dance

A certain girl, Mary, was popular. She was likeable. She was tall for her age. Within a crowd of girls, she seemed to stand out. Her hair was long. It flowed easily over her shoulders. She was attractive. She smiled easily. Friends. I liked her from a distance. She had the boys' attention.

She mostly danced with older boys. They made sure to be close to her in between dances. I was determined to dance with her. I hung within striking distance with older boys. We had the same idea. Even when I danced with someone else, I kept my eye on Mary. I almost missed by waiting too long for a dance with Mary. The last dance of the night was announced. It was a slow dance; it always was a slow dance.

I joined other boys as we approached her. Mary looked in my direction. I flashed her a smile. I had her attention. The music began. She reached for my hands. We were dancing close. We didn't say anything. I was in ya-ya land.

The Platters, a very popular group in the fifties, were singing their number one recording, "The Great Pretender." Mary G. smiled as we danced. Personally, I was in ya-ya land, still. We were eye-to-eye. She was as tall as me. Her cologne was magical. My arm encircled her soft waist.

The song ended. Couples were separating from each other. We remained on the dance floor before walking off holding hands. She was gone. Just like that; she was gone. I was barely under control. Dancing with Mary proved to be overwhelming. My gonads exploded. I limped back to my dormitory. Geez!

Iris

I did have a girlfriend. 'Iris' was Spanish. She was young and very pretty. We were attracted to each other. I'm assuming we were. We'd attend Saturday movies in Tottenville, I even initiated her name on my left forearm, with a razor blade; not deep enough for it to remain visible. No guts! We'd search different areas on the campus grounds where we could be alone. Hylan Boulevard provided a mid-point for us. We huddled behind a square cement pillar just off the boulevard on the girl's side of The Mount. We'd spend as much time as possible hugging, kissing, and occasionally dry humping. What!

Messages

Flashlights signaled messages in code, albeit simple messages between both sides of dormitories facing across from each other. Written messages between both sides were also exchanged. Boys and girls who had access to each side were carrier messengers. Messages via flashlights were simple codes flashing on and off. Using names in code. Saturday dates and Friday night dance requests. Very cool!

Chapter Three

Mom Is Alive

We were into our seventh year at The Mount. Al was told by a social worker that Mom was alive. Al told Bob and me. Mom was alive. Whoa! "Mom's alive?" "Where is she? Wait." Dad told us Mom was gone as he casually passed out photos of Mom and us. "Mom is alive." We believed she was dead. "Dad said so." I recall him saying it. What the hell!

Dad's communication with us was non-existent. Thinking back, it was easy. We were young and trusting. We didn't ask questions. Did we miss signals? Were we the only ones? What roles did aunts, uncles, and grandparents play? Did Mom know we were placed in an orphanage? I was upset.

Being told Mom was alive, in our seventh year at The Mount, renewed confusion and questions. Dad found out that we knew Mom was alive. His reaction was, do what he did best. He ignored our questions.

We were caught in the middle. We weren't capable of doing very much. Dad continued visiting and behaving as though nothing was wrong. On a visit with aunts, uncles, grandpa, and grandma, I learned from Grandma Mom visited them in their apartment. "Your Mother was a nice lady," was all Grandma said. Now, it was out in the open. All of us knew Mom was alive and committed to the mental ward facility in Bellevue hospital.

Al, Bob, and me served two authorities. The Mount's policies and regulations and Dad's overwhelming influence. In Dad's case, his hold over us was slowly being challenged. In time, armed with news that Mom was alive we resolved to reach out to her. Dad's lifestyle was interrupted and challenged. His relationship with Aunt Dolly was compromised. Mom was the 'Elephant in the room.'

Meeting Mom

Social workers arranged for Al to visit Mom. His initial visit with her was interesting, to say the least. He arrived at Brooklyn State Mental facility. He was directed to Mom's ward. In Al' words. Mom was confined to a wooden chair. She was wrapped in a straitjacket. Al identified himself to the attendant. He was told Mom was in a fight with another resident. The attendant released Mom from the straitjacket.

She looked up at Al. Her first words were. "Hi, Al." What the hell. It had been the better part of seven years since she laid eyes on him; on any of us for that matter. Mom was calm, talkative, and in control. *In control!* Are you kidding me? Geez!

I was next to visit Mom. I was alone. I was anxious. Actually, I was a nervous wreck. I arrived at the hospital. The building was dark, old, and looked used. I approached a large counter. It was crowded with people, standing, talking, asking questions. I was given Mom's floor and directed to a group of large elevators. I squeezed in between adults, visitors, nurses, and patients in their gowns. I was stared at. Why not, I was all of fifteen years old, small, thin, nervous, and looked younger than my age.

The large elevator doors opened. I stepped out into a large and open ward. There was a hum of loud voices, laughter from patients throughout the ward. A few patients were walking toward me.

I spotted Mom before they reached me. Thankfully, Mom wasn't in a straitjacket. She was sitting with a few friends in an open area. She looked in the direction of the elevator. She recognized me. She stood up. She smiled that smile of hers of so many years before. Her smile was accompanied with a sadness in her eyes. I was helpless.

Mom

Mom was diagnosed by medical doctors as sycophantic paranoid and declared incurably insane. She endured just short of eleven years, in and out of the confines of Brooklyn State Hospital's Mental Facility.

Mom was born August 30, 1919 to Rosaline and Alphonse Fiorillo. She was baptized November 9, 1919 at Our Lady of Peace Church at 522 Carroll

Street Brooklyn, New York. Mom received the Sacrament of Matrimony to Dominic Gaudioso on May 23, 1938.

She gave birth to three sons. Alphonse born August 23, 1938; John born January 5, 1940; followed by Robert, born January 14, 1941, one year and nine days after John's birth.

Following 10 years of marriage to Dad, Mom was committed to Brooklyn State Hospital's Mental Facility. Throughout almost eleven years, Mom was exposed to isolation from her family, most damaging her three young boys; Al, John, and Robert. Confinement, medical treatments, experimental drugs available at the time and loneliness.

Leaving The Mount

It felt weird! We were leaving friends. We'd learned to juggle a life completely devoid of family influences. Our new family consisted of priests, sisters, Xavier Brothers, and counselors. They provided steerage needed and enforced throughout our years in The Mount. 'A Few Good Years' in Brooklyn became distant memories.

We left The Mount as abruptly as we arrived, eight plus years earlier. We were unprepared then; we were unprepared again. We'd known confusion, tears, loneliness, disappointments, and the unanswered question, "What did we do wrong?"

Throughout the week, I made the rounds saying good-byes to friends. I emptied my bedroom drawer of stuff and clothes from my closet. I gave away cigarettes, shirts, jeans, a jacket, and a pair of shoes. I wandered to the small side, where it all began for me and my brothers. I peeked into the gymnasium. I was met with patters of basketballs bounding off backboards. No one paid me any attention; I was just another boy from the big side.

I exited the gymnasium. I walked to the rear of the gym. Memories of being caught smoking came to mind. I walked the playground slope where I thrilled to roller skating in a train of boys hurling toward the open trench separating the playground from the cottages. It was one hell of a ride.

I walked alongside the cottages on the small side where Al, Bob, and I were housed. I felt nothing! Little boys looked in my direction. Some looked confused. Others seem to be asking, "What did I do wrong?" As they grew older, they'll have learned to work 'the system.'

I walked toward Hylan Boulevard. A girl walked toward me. We didn't recognize each other, which wasn't unusual. Boys and girls ran in different groups. Her name was Carol. We joined together, walking and talking.

She was at The Mount just over two years. We were about the same age. She thought she knew me. It felt comfortable to be speaking with her, knowing it was going to be a brief encounter. Why wouldn't it be? Two teenagers, each with thoughts and reasons known only to ourselves. I didn't tell her I was leaving The Mount. No reason to.

Here We Go Again

A few years after receiving the news that Mom was alive, Dad announced we were leaving The Mount. Being underage, with Dad having parental responsibility for us, weather we agreed or not, we were going home to live with him and Aunt Dolly.

Dad and Aunt Dolly were married. Dad was in his own world. We were in a quandary. Dad's attempt to unite Aunt Dolly and us into a family was doomed to fail.

It was uncomfortable for Al, Bob, and me. Things became sticky. Years of planning by Dad to establish a family was wishful thinking on his part. For one, he didn't count on Mom resurfacing. Secondly, he assumed it was OK to keep his three boys out of the loop. We were used. We had no idea what role we were being positioned for. Everyone else seemed to be in the know! Maybe, a script would have eased us into playing our parts in their lives. At any rate, Dad's years of emphasizing positioning, control, and influencing us was coming apart at the seams.

Reconnecting

In spite of living with Dad, we managed to reach out to Mom's family. We were welcomed with open arms. We established a routine; visiting Mom at Bellevue hospital plus visits with aunts and other family members.

Dad wasn't pleased. Aunt Dolly was beside herself. She was angry. At times, she lost control. She stammered, yelling at Dad. She overnighted at her sister's house. Could 'The Men in White' be far behind? The situation was cloudy. We were caught between Dad, Aunt Dolly, Mom, and ourselves. We had a Mom and she was alive. Little by little, we learned to ignore Dad's outbursts.

We committed to living with Dad until graduating from high school. In the meantime, we tried not to upset the apple cart. Dad and Aunt Dolly on one side; Al, Bob and me, continuing our journeys.

Dad didn't interfere with our reuniting relationship with Mom. That in itself had to be difficult. We continued seeing Mom whenever arrangements could be made with her family. Mom made it easy to be with her. She never, ever complained. She never mentioned Dad. Her weekends away from the hospital calmed her. Leaving Mom to return to Dad's house and her return to the hospital ward had to be difficult for her; it was for us.

Aunt Dolly

Was Aunt Dolly duped; taken advantage of by Dad's considerable influence? You begin to understand his influence by her agreeing to a family environment completely opposite from the one she was raised in. On the other hand, what in the world convinced her that knowing our Mom was alive, she could replace her?

What was Dad thinking? Aside from Mom being sick, weren't options available in handling her illness while continuing to keep three young children together as a family? Isn't it strange; Dad returned to a local dance hall where he met Mom? Isn't it strange Dad met Aunt Dolly at a local dance hall? Was Dad committed to giving up on Mom a foregone conclusion?

Meeting Aunt Dolly, as our Aunt Dolly was the first introduction of mudding the waters. The second and the most important mistake was Dad sharing photos of Mom with us; He told us, "Mom was sick." Before leaving, he told us "Mom was gone." Up to that point, we hadn't a clue as to what happened to Mom. With Mom contained in Bellevue's mental facility, and us several years into an orphanage, we played into Dad's hand. He had opportunities to move on with his life. His influence over us was doomed. We had no issues with that. Thanks, Dad.

Aunt Dolly arrived with Dad each time he visited us. She arrived with fried chicken, candy, and smiles. We were OK meeting Aunt Dolly. Why not? She was nice to us. We accepted her as a part of our family. In our eyes, she was an aunt; nothing more, nothing less.

Within a few weeks living with Dad and Aunt Dolly, things began to sour between us. Aunt Dolly didn't have a clue how to raise three teenagers. We marched to own beat of drums. Our attitudes really changed when Dad made it clear we were to call Aunt Dolly 'mom.' It wasn't gonna happen. Not in a million years.

We weren't exposed to a family upbringing. The Mount replaced our family. We were exposed to their rules and regulations. Eight plus years in an orphanage will do that. Things were going south, fast. We adjusted as best we could.

With Mom in our lives, again; it wasn't long before Dad and Aunt Dolly were out of sorts with us. We visited Mom, reunited with aunts and uncles. We were welcomed into their homes. It was natural for us to be reunited with Mom and her family. As for Dad and Aunt Dolly; all of us were uncomfortable. Mom was the elephant in the room.

Dad lied to us. Mom wasn't dead. He was in a pickle. Aunt Dolly was trying to figure out how to deal with three boys. Dad's attitude? He was the father. He didn't need to discuss his reasoning or decisions concerning us and Mom. When pressed, he replied. "You wouldn't understand." *Try us.*

Moving Out and About

One by one, we completed high school and moved on. Al was kicked out of the house three times. Aunt Dolly requested Al back twice. Tossed out the third time and welcomed back again; Al refused. He entered a monastery. Ouch! He left after a year or two; enlisting in the Air Force. Yea! Bob sized up his situation as fast as he could. After graduating from high school, he enlisted in the Army. He returned to live with his high school sweetheart, Rose Marie. Eventually they were married.

I graduated from high school. I was ill-equipped to deal with academic challenges. Within hours following graduation, I was playing stick ball while other kids were off to summer vacations and or planning for colleges in the fall. Others looked forward to attending colleges in the fall. I didn't have a plan. I enlisted in the Air Force.

In between our paradigms we continued visiting with Mom. Al arranged military leave and flew Mom to Miami where they stayed with Aunt Rae, Mom's older sister and her husband, Tom. Mom received visits from her sisters and brothers. Our Aunt Helen, Uncle Dom, and their daughters visited Mom on Sundays with Mom's favorite pasta meals. Aunt Helen's daughters, Rosanne and Roxanne, were too young to visit their Aunt Anna. They remained in the car parked in the street, in front of the hospital.

Mom waved to them from a window in her ward. Rosanne once remarked to Aunt Helen, "That Aunt Anna was prettier than Sofia Loren." When Mom heard what was said, she glowed. Mom was beautiful. I'd be remiss if I didn't acknowledge Mom's family members, sisters, brothers, brother- and sister-in-laws. They contributed to Mom's needs as best they were able to.

Mom's Quest for Independence
1961 – 1964

According to hospital records, Mom began showing interest in rehabilitation. Following a series of monitored supervision, she was considered capable of caring for herself. She applied for and received convalescence status on September 20, 1961 with a stipulation, releasing her to the care and supervision of her sisters. For a while she resided with a sister, Mary, living at 5 Berkley Place, Brooklyn, and NY. She was provided a clinic appointment card, directing her to monthly check up visits. She was making progress that after eleven years was remarkable.

After a short amount of time, Mom rented a small one-room apartment on Carroll Street, not far from her sister. The hospital put her in touch with The Williams Employment Agency. An interview was arranged with Eagle Electric Company. Mom was hired as an assembler.

*Records indicate Dad was ordered by the courts to pay into a Brooklyn State savings account, (441.250-8) a big twenty-three dollars a week. I assume Mom had access. Al and I assisted Mom with her expenses on a monthly basis from our military salaries.

For several months, her convalescence was good. But, as time passed, she was managing a full-time job and her own household. Her adjustments to living outside the hospital began to test her ability to focus on her assignment as an assembler. Mom struggled coping with the realities of living on her own.

She became affected by life's demands. Her inability to concentrate on her job led to losing her job. She remained in her apartment.

Case workers followed up with Mom on a monthly basis. Follow up reviews indicated Mom showed little interest in returning to regular work. Hospital documents state Mom's thinking became more and more unrealistic. She wasn't able to accept the fact her husband divorced her. She suffered from isolation and an inability to cope with responsibilities. It got to a point where Mom requested to return to the hospital. She wanted to be with her friends. They were her family.

Adjustments Again!

In an effort to compensate for Mom's emotional ups and downs, family members, mainly her sisters, visited and often bought her to their homes for visits. Unfortunately, they witnessed Mom's highs and lows throughout many years confined to a mental ward. Mom was treated for schizophrenic, paranoid Type. All of which, along with other accepted varieties of treatments in the early years, influenced her recovery. My opinion.

Mom's Request

A letter dated June 17, 1963 was written and addressed to The Red Cross and the U. S. Air Force by Mom.

To whom it may concern:

I'm the mother of a 2/c John Gaudioso. I request that he be given a compassionate discharge from the Air Force because I am urgently in need of his help at home.

I became ill when he was a child and was a patient at Brooklyn State Hospital for 11 years. At the time he was enlisted, I was undergoing rehabilitation and job training and expected to be able to manage. His father secured a divorce in 1955. So I have lived alone since I left the hospital on September 20, 1961.

I have been so disturbed that I am sick with loneliness, and am not able to work while I am so upset. It is vital for me to have some family life and I need my son with me.

I do earnestly beseech that my son be granted a discharge.

Mom's letter was accompanied by three additional letters, restating her wishes as written in her letter to the Red Cross and the U.S. Air Force.

Mom's initial illness, April 13, 1947, was diagnosed with the disease, schizophrenia, paranoid Type. Subsequently, she was declared incurably insane by Brooklyn State Hospital medical staff. In ensuing years, she appeared to take a turn for the better, the result of rehabilitation and job training. She requested and was granted a convalescent leave by the medical staff at Brooklyn State Hospital.

Hospital Recommendations

The following are taken from a confidential report from the medical department at Bellevue Hospital, dated, July 8, 1963. Mom's early adjustment while on convalescent status was quite good. She lived in her own apartment. The following report summarizes findings by the medical staff:

"Nine to ten months ago, increasing evidence began to manifest itself that the patient's adjustment outside the hospital was trending to lapse. She had lost her job and showed little inclination to return to regular work. Her thinking became more and more unrealistic. For instance, she was unable to accept the fact that she had been divorced by her husband, and that the latter had remarried. She felt very much alone, and complained about this.

"There were times when she preferred to return to the hospital, rather than live in her own apartment, mainly because she had friends here. Unfortunately, the members of her family closest to her, such as her sisters, and sons, either show no interest in her predicament, or were living a great distance from her, and were unable to give her any emotional support.

"The possibility that her son, John, might be discharged from the air force for compassionate reasons would appear to be a factor that will probably be of great benefit to her in bolstering her morale, and maintaining her under normal conditions outside the hospital."

Compassionate Honorable Discharge

On July 19, 1963, the Director of Military Personnel directed the field Director of the American Red Cross to forward the request discharging me from the military, a compassionate discharge under honorable conditions.

Prior to my discharge, granted August 23, 1963, I was summoned to meet with Father John, my Chaplin. What did I do now? Father John and I shared history. I managed to get into a scrap in downtown Seville. Duh! The Military

Air Police were summoned to the La Guardia police station, where I was being made comfortable! Fortunately, an air policeman recognized me. I'd taken Christmas photos of him for his family. I received a personal escort to my dorm room. The door was opened. I was tossed inside. Charges were leveled against me. Father John intervened on my behalf.

I was confined to operational responsibilities. I was restricted to base for thirty days. Father John monitored my progress. I was on a short leash. I was assigned to the choir. When it became obvious I couldn't carry a tune, I was moved to the last row of the choir and told to hum.

Father John reviewed documents requesting I be granted a compassionate discharge to be with Mom. The Red Cross forwarded their support of her request. We discussed the pros and cons. I explained my reluctance to leave the Military service (self-serving).

Mom's illness was a major concern. Was I prepared to deal with her mental illness? What were her medications? Was I entering into something I'd regret or worst, couldn't handle? Memories of early years ultimately played a role in my decision. Being separated for close to 16 years weighed heavily on me. We lived in different worlds. My head was spinning.

I had very little information – almost none from the hospital, regarding the depth of her illness, other than the original diagnostic findings! Mom was schizophrenic paranoid and declared incurably insane. Was I tackling something beyond my reach? I didn't have answers. I was confused, again!

After thinking and reviewing what my brothers and I were hit with, growing up in an orphanage, it hit me like a ton of bricks. Mom was dealt a bad hand. I agreed to the hardship discharge. My decision wasn't without doubts. Al and Bob had done more than their share visiting and being with Mom in my early years while deployed overseas. I wrote Dad of my decision to leave the military to be with Mom. He didn't respond – no surprise there!

Entering Uncharted Waters
August 23, 1963

I caught a flight out of Seville, Spain, with a connection through The Azores before continuing to McGuire Air Force Base, in New Jersey. I was mustered out of the military the following day, along with large group of personnel from various branches of the military.

The route to Carroll Street, Brooklyn, provided me an awareness of things that changed in my three years stationed overseas. It felt strange traveling in full uniform negotiating buses, trains, and subways. My stomach was bundled in knots. As I neared Mom's apartment, a group of girls fell in behind me. They serenaded me, singing a popular tune, *Soldier Boy.* Was I really ready for this next phase of my life?

Soldier Boy
Moving in with Mom

Arrival

I wish it was more dramatic – "Hi Mom." It wasn't. Mom opened the door to my knocks. We stared at each other, is this happening? We hugged. We stood apart. We hugged again.

I entered Mom's apartment. I placed my duffle bag down, taking in the surroundings. It hit me. The strangeness and the realization of it all. 'Discharged from the military. Arriving at Mom's apartment. Nothing prearranged.' What!

Mom's appearance set me back just for a moment or two. She paid a toll, mentally and physically. It was unsettling for me. The first moments passed. Mom began apologizing for not preparing for my arrival. She offered me her room, as small as it was. I assured her the couch was fine, for the time being. She offered me whatever space I needed in her room to stow my belongings. I had my duffle bag.

Mom didn't seem to be listening. She began emptying drawers, explaining, she would move her things elsewhere. I explained my things wouldn't arrive for the next few days. We were fine for the time being. There wasn't much in the way of furniture, a small T.V. on top of a small chest. A single chair in the corner next to an end table. It was OK.

Over the next days, we settled in. Mom and I settled into a routine. Our first days were spent catching up. Just becoming comfortable with each other. My attempts to revisit events experienced by us and my brothers were generally met with casual comments. She'd asked about Al and Bob. I explained what they were up to. She'd smile. She didn't seem interested beyond small chitchat. At times, she seemed distracted.

We settled into a routine. Shopping for groceries together, watching T.V. programs, and walks throughout the neighborhood. Her friends began to stop over. With them, she would, at times, become her old self, laughing about things they shared in common. The refrigerator was stocked with cold cuts and cheeses. Cereals and canned goods were stored on shelves. Our first night, we ate Chinese at a local restaurant.

In the Interim
Bob and Rose Marie's Wedding

They invited Mom. Dad didn't attend. No loss. Unfortunately, Al and I weren't available to attend. We were both deployed while serving in the military.

Mom attended their wedding invitation. Rose Marie's Dad, Ralph, picked Mom up at the Hospital and returned her to the hospital after the wedding. Ralph and Jean were a wonderful, caring couple.

Uncles and aunts from Dad's side of the family showed in force to the wedding. Seeing Mom in attendance stunned them. Bob relates, "Mom was radiant. She was the Belle of the Ball." She danced with several uncles – Dad's brothers. One uncle remarked to Bob. "What was your dad thinking?" I'll let that go unchallenged. Bob and Rose Marie? A class act.

Mom, Rose Marie, and Bob.
Bob and Rose Marie's Wedding

Mom dancing with Uncle Pete

As previously agreed to, I called Bob once I settled in. They visited Mom's apartment. I was wired tight. Hopefully, they didn't notice. Mom was also wired, chatting non-stop. It was great hooking up with Bob and Rose Marie. Their presence went a long way in relaxing me. They helped with my unpacking. We stored stuff here and there, searching for space in both rooms. Bob and Rose Marie's visit was too short for me. Spending time with them, seeing them leave, left me with an empty feeling. They were married. Al was in the military. I was with Mom.

Mom's days were easy enough to adjust to. As time passed, Mom's friends dropped over routinely. In good weather, they'd take walks or have lunch together. I made sure Mom had a few dollars. I needed to search for employment. I didn't have a car. It came down to public transportation, buses, and trains. I was living off mad money, accumulated from unused vacations while in the military.

My search for employment dragged into weeks. My savings were low. Mom depended on a small amount of money from the state from an account set in her name in Brooklyn State Hospital. It didn't amount to much. I suspect she may have received assistance from her family. My years in the military prepared me to a lifestyle according to rules and regulations. Now, returned to civilian life, I needed to adjust to a life-style 'outside of the box.'

I made the rounds to employment agencies. There were a few positions offered with my photographic background and experience. I came to grips with it. I moved on. I repeated visits to employment agencies. I had a nibble for a job at The World's Fair grounds, in Flushing Meadows. An interview was arranged with a private contractor. I found the office. It was a shack in the middle of a lot, filled with garbage trucks.

A few-back-and-forth questions. He explained he had contracts hauling garbage from trash bins located behind concessions stands at The World's Fair, in Flushing Meadows. I'd be paid in cash. No paper work to sign off on. The money was good. He offered me a job. I was in. Cool!

I reported to the opened lot each morning. I was assigned to a crew. Our trucks circled the rear of the concession stands; we emptied garbage from large bins into our trucks. The garbage was transferred to our lot. The collected trash was weighed before being driven by different drivers to another dump, somewhere in Queens. No questions asked. None were expected.

Sometimes, after completing a job early, we'd stop in a bar for a few beers. These guys were a different breed. Foul language was a second language to them. They consumed lots of beer. I couldn't keep up with them. I was the 'kid' recently discharged from the military and living with his mom. Sports was the accepted subject, baseball, football, hockey, and basketball, oh yeah, and boasting about broads was a close second.

As mom and I got to know each other better, never referring to Dad, I was aware she was told of Dad's divorce from her by the medical staff at Brooklyn State Hospital. She didn't seem interested in discussing our times living in Brooklyn either. She didn't bring up or show an interest with our upbringing in The Mount. Any attempts may have been too painful for Mom. She seemed content with things just the way they were.

She didn't discuss her illnesses. She did emphasize she'd completed a rehabilitation program. But, nothing beyond that. Mostly, our conversations were light. She didn't remain on any subject for a long period of time. The exception being her times with her friends. For the most part, Mom's friendships were a blessing for her. Many were on temporary convalescent leave from the hospital. Their conversations were minimal in my presence.

They were cordial. Nevertheless, I was 'the elephant in the room.' I'd excuse myself. I enjoyed long walks throughout a neighborhood I felt I was intruding. Aside from occasional takeout from the neighborhood Chinese restaurant, we mostly ate at home. Mom usually prepared meals. The lone exception was Sunday pasta and meatballs. Mom took care of our cleaning. She walked to the local Laundromat which was just down the block. Short walks together were mostly in silence and enjoyable.

Mom Wasn't Right!

A few months passed before Mom began complaining of an upset stomach. At first, I thought it might have something to do with her not eating properly at lunch. She assured me she was. Sundays, we relaxed. Mom listening to the radio. Smoking a cigarette, smiling as I prepared our Sunday meal. Meatballs, tomato gravy, and pasta. Mom loved her pasta. I made enough to reheat leftovers for lunch. By the time I returned from work on a Monday, the left-over pasta and meatballs were gone. As for other meals, she seemed to pick at them, often not finishing her meal. I knew something was brewing.

I let it pass. Our conversations improved. She enjoyed listening to my day at work. I described the 'stuff' dumped in trash bins. Mostly leftover food, empty bottles, and plastic containers. She wanted to know about the cats that hung around the trash bins. She asked if I could bring her a cat. I said I'd try to catch one.

We smoked while watching the evening news. Mom usually put up a cup of tea. I had a beer. That pretty much described our evenings. I'd hit the couch. I had to be up early for work. Mom headed to her room to watch T.V. I was up and gone before she was up. A short ride on the subway, a stop for a regular coffee and buttered roll and I was ready for another day of making the rounds picking up trash from concessions.

Overtime

Following our last run, rotated crews cleaned trucks, preparing them for the following day's runs. Mom wasn't comfortable with me working late. Occasionally I was able to swap out with someone. I didn't mind working beyond my normal day. In any case, I'd get home as soon as possible. In the beginning, Mom was OK. Eventually, she depended on me arriving home after a normal day's work. Mom was concerned being in the apartment alone at night.

When I worked beyond my shift, I suggested that Mom turn up the volume on the TV set; hopefully to calm her nerves. I'm sure the neighbors heard the TV loud and clear as sometimes Mom turned the volume up very loud.

When I returned home and climbed the stairs to her apartment, if I didn't hear the TV, it meant one of two things. Either one of her girlfriends was talked into staying with her until I arrived home, or she was across the hallway with the next-door neighbor. After checking our apartment and finding it empty, I'd knock and enter her neighbor's apartment. Mom was waiting with a smile for me.

Her neighbors were nice enough. The guy drove a cab. He was large with a gruff profile. He wasn't talkative. He usually watched T.V. or read a newspaper. When he did speak from a kitchen-table chair, he voiced complaints about how things were going to the dogs in the city. His wife stood off to the side, often with her hands wrapped around a cloth or fumbling her fingers, smiling at me. Their daughter stood behind her, also smiling. Weird!

Living with Mom wasn't as smooth as I'd liked it to be. There were awkward moments. But, it was doable. My attempts at recalling memories when we lived in Brooklyn fell flat. Mom avoided discussing family members, except when her sisters' names were mentioned. They remained close to her. They provided loving care and support for her. They were there for Mom from the very beginning, supporting her illnesses throughout her enduring treatments while confined to a mental facility.

Monthly Care Visits

Part of Mom's release required her to attend monthly care visits with her medical team. I was included in her care visits. Mom knew how to handle questions by staff members. When she was focused, she was a smart cookie. When asked if she was ready to return to work, she responded, "I'm feeling better, but not yet." Mom had no intention of returning to work. We discussed our time together, her friends visiting, and other small talk. As always, after the group review, we were separately counseled.

I responded to the usual questions. 'How was she reacting to our living arrangement?' 'Was I comfortable with the arrangement?' 'Was Mom receiving visits from family members?' 'Did I have concerns?' I did.

I mentioned Mom being uncomfortable when I'd work overtime. She didn't like to be alone. I reviewed steps taken by me in reassuring Mom. I brought up Mom's complaints of stomach issues and her lack of appetite. We agreed, I'd contact them if the issues continued. I continued to monitor Mom's concerns. Her complaining of stomach discomfort continued. Her appetite was poor. She was nervous and jumpy. I mentioned my concerns to the medical team on our next care visit. They agreed to readmit her for further examinations, specifically related to her stomach discomfort. Mom's concerns were that she be returned to her apartment. They agreed. Mom was on board, not that she had a choice!

A Turning Point

It gets a bit blurry here. The Hospital addressed a WESTERN UNION telegram to me. The problem – it was mailed to Dad's address. Why? The hospital had my address which was Mom's apartment! I contacted Dad, requesting the telegram.

JOHN GAUDIOSO
853 Oaks Drive Franklin Square NY
CONSENT FOR PARACENTHESIS ON ANNA GAUDIOSO
KINDLY CONTACT HOSPITAL IMMEDIATELY
BROOKLYN STATE HOSPITAL
XXXXXXXXXXX MD DIRECTOR

I contacted the medical staff and consented to the surgery for Mom. Surgery revealed a large amount of accumulated fluid in her stomach. Mom was returned to her hospital ward. A drainage tube was inserted into her abdomen to collect fluids from her stomach into a pail.

The outlook for Mom wasn't encouraging. She wouldn't be coming back to her apartment. Just in case, she was cleared to return to her apartment, I arranged for her belongings to be stored with a family member. Mom never returned to her apartment.

Al was unable to visit Mom. He was serving in the military. Bob was married, attending college, and positioning a career path. Bob and I settled into a routine. We visited Mom on Saturday, together or separately. Visits were difficult. Upon entering the hospital, we joined residents, hanging in and about the lobby, some waiting for visitors, others just wandering.

Riding in a large elevator filled with staff, residents, and visitors was interesting and uncomfortable. Each elevator stop, before reaching Mom's ward, opened to another group of staff, residents, and visitors, waiting for the elevator. Behind them, voices and admonitions cried out throughout the ward. Staff, residents, and visitors piled out, replaced by staff, residents, and visitors piling in. No one spoke.

Observation. Our efforts reaching out to Mom pulled us together. Whereas the years spent in The Mount, to some degree, had the opposite effect.

Dad Visits Mom

Mom was dying. Mom's oldest sister Aunt Rae appeared at Dad's home. She and Dad spoke outside the house. She demanded Dad to visit Mom. It was ironic; Dad visiting Mom at Bellevue Hospital many years after signing her into the facility.

Dad knew Bob and I visited Mom on Saturdays. He asked me if he could join us. I outright refused him. He countered, "I don't know the way." How could he not know the way? I was pissed. I reminded him, he knew the way when he had Mom committed. That was the end of our relationship. We didn't communicate for almost six years. He visited Mom. Bob and I arranged to arrange to visit Mom after Dad left.

Mom spotted us as we exited the elevator. She shouted, "Dominic was here. He came to see me," Mom was sitting with friends in the middle of their ward. A drainage tube emptied fluids from her stomach into a pail. She was dying. Dominic visited her. Mom never stopped loving Dad. I wonder. What could he have done differently? Geez.

Mom Passed Away

Mom passed away October 11, 1964. She was forty-four years old. She died alone, in a bed, set up against a green wall in a room just off the ward. Bob and I arrived at the hospital. We briefly met with a doctor and a nurse before we were escorted to a private room. Mom was being prepared for the transfer to a funeral home. Mom was so innocent. I didn't say the words at the time. Today, I'm still confused... Why! Why did it had to be this way?

I contacted Aunt Helen and Uncle Dom. Funeral arrangements were discussed. They assured me funeral expenses would be taken care of. Four hundred dollars remaining in Mom's account with the greater New York Savings Bank was released to me. It was the amount deposited by Dad toward Mom's funeral expenses, ordered in his annulment from her on June 1, 1961. I endorsed it over to Uncle Dom and Aunt Helen.

It was included in the actual burial cost; one thousand, seven hundred and ninety dollars. Uncle Dom and Aunt Helen's financial arrangements for Mom's funeral were transparent to us. We can never thank them enough. They were there for us. To this day, Aunt Helen and Uncle Dom remain an important part in my life.

Mom was waked at Joseph J. Russo Funeral Home, in Brooklyn, N.Y. Al arranged leave from his military base. Bob, Rose Marie, and I attended. Mom's wake along with her close family members. Floral arrangement including one from Dad arrived with an attached card, from Dom and the Boys. What the hell! I'll leave it at that.

Mom was laid to rest in Saint Charles Commentary, Farmingdale, on Long Island. She was placed in Uncle Dom and Aunt Helen's family plot under the name of Spadafina. Mom's name 'Anna Rose Gaudioso' was added at a later date.

Mom
Anna Rose Fiorillo
Teenager

"IN LOVING MEMORY OF MOM"

GARDENS OF THE WORLD
Founded by the Hogan Foundation
THOUSANDS OAKS, CALIFORNIA

Photo of John, Bob, and Al
1947

Mom inscribed this photo to us
prior to our reunion.

I see Mom, I hear her, I feel her presence
as I experienced them
throughout a few good years.

John, Al, Bob. Jim, Lena Finamore, and Grandpa

Confirmations?

Al, Dad, John, Bob
"Three suits to be returned."

Bob, Al, John

John's graduation from grammar school 1952
Al, Uncle Frank, Tony Milano
Bob, John, and Grandpa

Epilogue

This manuscript contains recollections true to what transpired throughout times of confusion, isolation, and challenges to Mom; my brothers Al, Bob, and me. Three weeks was compiled over many years dealing with draft copies, revisions, and frustrating recollections.

Was Mom really able to care for herself? Could it have been too much to expect of her? Did her release do her more harm than good? Were her monthly care visits timely and productive valuations? Was Mom's release based on reducing in-house care to patients, due to budgetary constraints? Just saying!

Somewhere deep in her past, maybe, lurking within her DNA make-up, before she met Dad; was she a ticking time bomb? Mom's illness was triggered by something? Reviewing available documents, I can't come close to an answer.

Once interned in Bellevue Hospital, Mom was subjected to medical treatments and sameness over many years. She fell in line with routines contributing within and relating to surrounding influences.

Was Mom a victim of "Stockholm Syndrome?" Throw in paranoid schizophrenia, and you have a dangerous recipe for hopelessness. Did the system beat her down? Consider years of enduring medical treatments, isolation, the loss of children, family members, and friendships. Add regimental exposure to routines associated with her treatments, and you begin to draw images of confinement to a mental institution.

Add personal adjustments dealing with confusion, depression, loss of decision-making, and enforced compliance, all playing major roles. Was Mom partnered into a system alone or with groupings of residents forced into compliance via drugs? Just wondering.

Once freed from the orphanage, we reached out her. It was too little, too late. We couldn't make up for lost years between Mom and us. She wasn't our 'Mommy'; 'we weren't her children.'

Thanks, Dad.

Post Years
John, Bob, and Al

Al

United States Air Force
Medic – US Based

Education

SUNY – BUFFALO
BS, OCC
STOUT State University

Master's Degree
UTAH-State-University
Master's Degree
Mondell Institute

Career

VR Counselor at Helen Hayes Hospital
Director of VR Department
Rockland Rehab agencies

Interests

Theatre, Opera, Ballet, Plays, Gardening, Family
A caring Uncle to nieces and nephews. Pets: Rocky *"Cat in charge"*

John

United States Air Force
Photographic Air – lab
Strategic Air Command

Education

Maryland University
La Salle University
AA Degree – Business
BS Duel Degrees – Marketing and
Commerce
Keller Management Group

Career

Transportation industry – forty-two years
Airlines – Car Rental – Pleasant Hawaiian Holidays
U.S. assignments – Overseas assignments
High School – Intervention Counselor

Family

Spouse: Jo Anne – Children – Nine Grandchildren
Interests: Author – Children's books – Memoir
Writing, Reading, Traveling, Gardening, Short naps

Bob

United States Army
Medic – US Based

Education

La Salle University
Marketing, Law, LLB

Career

Sun Oil Company – LIC --Avis Car Rental.
Franklin National Bank.
EAB International Bank
Founding Partner – Personal investments
Seminary – Ordained Deacon

Family

Spouse: Rose Marie – Children – Four Grandchildren
Interests: Serving communities – Reading – Family – Friendships
– Traveling – Golf – Baseball Team

John, Robert, Alphonse

Mom